Kundalini Death Cure

The Magic of Micro Dosing DMT

WRITTEN BY

AARON BENSETTE

Published by Fretstorm Publishing
London

Written and designed by Aaron Bensette

ISBN 978-1-7387377-2-7

This book is dedicated to

our

Mother

Contents

CHAPTER 1 - MY INTRO

This is a book that has never been written.

The content presented within is the direct result of my personal experimentation, several years ago, with the psychedelic DMT. This is not a work of fiction. Although it may be nearly impossible for the reader to believe what I'm saying, I promise to give an honest and factual account of my experience, even when it is uncomfortable to do so.

It has been difficult for me to write this because I am not a writer. I am a retired rock star, personal support worker, a cheese maker, and a hotel front desk clerk... but a writer, I am not. I don't have the wonderful words to describe a psychedelic experience as it should be described. It is also not easy to be completely open and honest about something as personal and private as the experience I will lay out later in this book.

I have delayed writing this book for two years because I didn't think I could do it. I questioned both my ability to write this and my ability to be completely honest. I spent a lot of time trying to figure out how to present everything in a way that made me look *smart* and *deep*. I wanted people to read my book and think I was a *great writer*.

I have this incredible method of using DMT that I want to tell the world about, but I just couldn't get past the first chapter. My need to impress people at the beginning got in the way of my getting to the important parts. Following many, many failed attempts to be *impressive*, I finally gave up on trying to be a *great writer* and accepted that I will only ever be just an average writer, with an incredible story to tell.

Since we are both eager to get to the good stuff that follows, this chapter will be as short as I can make it, but there are a few things that we need to discuss before we move on to the "how we do it" and "what happens when we do it" stages.

In 2016, purely by accident, I discovered a new, and very specific, technique of micro dosing DMT. Since then, I have realized this is a method that nobody else uses. It is not something I learned from the Internet or from someone else's published work. I have never found a psychedelic trip report that describes what I will be sharing with you. As far as I can tell, I am the only person who has ever documented this method of using DMT, and the incredible experience that follows.

Micro dosing DMT, let's call it MdDMT, is a brand new method of using DMT. Those who are already familiar with the world's most potent psychedelic are no doubt also aware of the two most common methods of use. It can be smoked in a pipe or swallowed as Ayahuasca.

Smoking or vaporizing pure DMT creates a mind-blowing 7 to 10 minute experience for the psychonaut. Ayahuasca, typically a drink mixture that contains DMT and an MAOi, is a much smoother and gentler experience that lasts considerably longer, perhaps 4 to 6 hours. Both methods often produce rich, life changing trips for the user.

These are the two most common methods of using DMT. One is smoked, and short in duration. The other is swallowed and lasts for several hours. There are many detailed trip reports, either written, or as videos, that have been shared by 21st Century explorers of psychedelia. If you are interested in further reading, just search the Internet for DMT trip reports and you'll find them.

I am presenting MdDMT as a new, third method of using DMT. While there are many individuals on the Internet who micro dose DMT, the method they typically describe is similar to the micro dosing strategy used with magic mushrooms; take a small amount every day for some number of days, perhaps even twice a day, and then present a trip report outlining what happened to them. While this is a successful method when using mushrooms (because they have a long lasting effect, often six to eight hours) this will not work for DMT. DMT is metabolized by the human body far too quickly for there to be any continuity of effect between doses. Successful micro dosing of DMT must occur at shorter time intervals to be an effective tool in one's psychedelic tool bag.

I'm sure you are now asking, "What is so special about this supposed *new* method of using DMT?" and "Why would anyone want to do it?" Simply put, the trip produced by MdDMT, is the exact same psychedelic experience, every time.

Let me say that again, as I know it sounds completely impossible. Using the technique of MdDMT, an explorer will have the same experience each time they do it. This may very well be the first time that those words have been used to describe any psychedelic experience.

There is a specific spiritual experience that lies within each human being. It's an experience that at one time long ago, was the primary method of achieving spiritual enlightenment and true expanded consciousness. Our ancient elders were masters at unlocking this extended DMT trip. They were very skilled at micro dosing DMT. MdDMT was the original method of achieving Ayahuasca, and although it was done in a different manner than we will use in the 21st Century, their more primitive method absolutely produced the exact same results that I'm presenting in this book.

Unfortunately, this original, powerful experience seems to have disappeared from the world's psychedelic menu. This is the most incredible experience a human being can have between birth and death, and it has been completely forgotten about by humanity. I intend to re-introduce this long lost experience to the world.

It's time for its return.

CHAPTER 2 - MY DISCOVERY

*M*icro dosing DMT is a very simple process once you understand how it works. It's a hybrid method that combines the convenience, purity, and strength of smoking pure DMT, with the gentler, longer lasting effects of traditional Ayahuasca.

Let's jump right in.

The first thing you need is DMT. The type of DMT is important. It must be the freebase version of *n,n dimethyltryptamine*. You can NOT use other variants of DMT, such as the *Bufo-Toad Venom*, or *5-meo DMT*. Do not assume that just any form of DMT will work. Make sure you use n,n DMT. It can range in color from white (which is very pure) to yellow/orange (which is less pure). Both purities will work equally well.

You will need an accurate digital scale that is sensitive enough to measure in milligrams. Weighing your DMT is critical.

The question of how much DMT is required leads to an answer that will certainly sound astonishingly huge to anyone familiar with the typical method of smoking DMT. A breakthrough dose is generally 50 - 60mg. Micro dosing DMT uses a considerable amount of the drug in one sitting. You need to have .5 grams (500mg) of DMT. You may not use all of it, but you do need to have it available.

Now for the warning: Do not have more than 500mg of DMT available. This is not a situation where more is better. Stick with 500mg and no more! Starting a session with more than the suggested amount will most likely get you in trouble. Starting with less is also not suggested. You need to allow for a small amount of waste, and you really don't want to run out prematurely. The perfect amount is 500mg. No more and no less.

The next item we need is a vaporizer. If you don't already own one, you'll need to get one. This is not a time to be cheap. You need a high quality tabletop vaporizer. It must include 2 glass bowls, a whip (the clear hose) and a mouthpiece.

At the time of writing this, I am aware of two companies that make vaporizers perfectly suited for MdDMT. Let's start with the well known "Volcano". This is the original tabletop vaporizer, and it has been around for 20 years. Unfortunately, its fantastic reputation comes with a hefty price tag, possibly putting it out of reach of many individuals. The other option is from Arizer. The specific model I recommend is the "Extreme Q". The kit includes everything you need and performs (in my opinion) as well as the Volcano, but it does so at 1/3 the price. Currently, in Canada, the price of an "Arizer Extreme Q" is $180.

The final item we need may be simple for many people but difficult or even impossible for others. We need something to act as a bed for the powdered DMT when it is placed in the vaporizer's bowl. The glass bowl will have a screen installed at the bottom, but we can't simply dump the DMT powder directly on the screen. When DMT is heated, it melts briefly before actually vaporizing and you can't allow the DMT to drip through the screen onto the heating element. Not only does this waste your DMT, but it will also ruin your expensive new vaporizer. I suggest pre-vaping a gram of marijuana beforehand. This will remove the THC from the pot, leaving you with relatively inert material that provides a perfect bed or base upon which to place the DMT. If you need to find another suitable substance to use as a bed or base, the Internet will provide additional alternatives. I have attempted to use tea leaves and dried mint myself, but both eventually ignite in the bowl and ruin everything.

With the DMT, a vaporizer, a scale, and something to act as a bed in the bowl, we have all we need. These four items will be everything you need to accomplish what follows.

To best illustrate what a session of micro dosing looks like in action, I will use a brief example.

Let's say our friend Bill has decided that he wants to try micro dosing DMT.

He sets up the vaporizer.

He loads a large amount of DMT into the glass bowl of the vaporizer.

He is ready to begin.

It is important to pay attention to the clock for this example. Let's assume that Bill begins at midnight.

At 0000 hrs, Bill takes a tiny hit (just a mouthful) of pure DMT from the vaporizer.

He tops his remaining breath off with room air, inhales it deeply, and counts silently in his head to 10 before finally exhaling it.

Immediately, Bill takes a second tiny hit of vapour and again tops the remainder of that breath off with room air.

Bill holds it in again, for a count of 10, before exhaling.

He repeats this "hit, top off, and hold" process a third time.

By 0001 hrs, Bill has taken 3 small hits in a row, but he is not done yet.

Bill will repeat this simple "hit, top off, and hold" process for 1 hour.

It should be noted that none of Bill's inhalations contain enough DMT to initiate an actual psychedelic experience. If Bill experiences any psychedelic effects following any single hit from the vaporizer, then he must be more careful and take a smaller hit next time. The goal is to NOT break through while micro dosing.

At 0030, half an hour has passed, and Bill continues taking his tiny sips of DMT vapour deep into his lungs. In fact, Bill has inhaled approximately 100 small hits of DMT in the last 30 minutes. Not once has he taken more than just a tiny sip of DMT. To do so would have launched a typical DMT trip and that is not the experience Bill is looking for tonight.

While we let Bill continue sipping his DMT, allow me to explain what I believe is happening to him at a chemical level. Bill's actions, although seemingly pointless, boring, and repetitive, are slowly reducing his body's available supply of *Monoamine Oxidase (MAO)*. Every time Bill inhales a tiny amount of DMT, a corresponding amount of his *MAO* is used up, or perhaps more accurately, burnt off.

It is now 0045 and Bill has not given up. He continues to take small sips of DMT, topping off each with room air.

Hit, top off, and hold
Hit, top off, and hold

Every breath is held for a count of 10. Every breath is slowly but surely depleting Bill's available supply of MAO. This is a good thing. This is the goal.

Let's consider traditional Ayahuasca for a moment. Thousands of people travel to South America every year for the sole purpose of experiencing Ayahuasca. Participants ingest a thick liquid that has been brewed for several hours. There are two ingredients in this brew. The first is

DMT, which provides the psychedelic portion of the experience. The second ingredient is an *MAOi*, or *Monoamine Oxidase Inhibitor*. The purpose of the MAO inhibitor is to temporarily shut down the body's production of MAO. This allows the swallowed DMT to become orally active, at which point, a psychedelic experience will begin. This unique combination of both DMT and the MAO inhibitor produces an extended DMT experience that is typically quite spiritually enlightening for those who do it. Unfortunately, Ayahuasca is also often accompanied by cramps, nausea, vomiting, and diarrhea, referred to as 'purging'. It is believed that feeling sickly, throwing up and shitting yourself is positive part of the Ayahuasca experience. You are releasing inner demons and freeing yourself from their grip. That is a belief shared by most of the Ayahuasca community. I don't know if that is true or not, but I do know that very few people want to vomit and shit uncontrollably, ever.

Micro dosing DMT will not make you puke or shit yourself and I personally think that's nice.

Now, back to Bill. He clearly understands that all DMT trips MUST be done on an empty stomach. If a person has any food in their stomach at the time of smoking DMT, they will vomit, and it is horrible. Just as you don't go on a roller coaster after eating, you need to respect this suggestion. Luckily, Bill read this book and took my advice.

In fact, Bill is almost done the task of sipping DMT. The time is now 0059 hrs and Bill has inhaled approximately

200 tiny hits of DMT. Over the course of one hour, Bill has gradually used up all his body's available supply of MAO.

At 0100 hrs, Bill finally can stop sipping DMT. He has just completed the 60 minute micro dosing portion of the experience.

At 0101 hrs, Bill takes what is commonly known as a breakthrough dose. He quickly smokes 60mg of DMT in 1 minute, and then gets comfortable.

Nothing happens... yet.

1 minute later and still nothing...

Suddenly, at 0103 hrs, Bill finds himself in another dimension!

There you go folks. That is how micro dosing DMT, or MdDMT, is done. One hour of sipping tiny amounts of DMT in every breath will gradually exhaust one's body of *Monoamine Oxidase (MAO)*. That hour is immediately followed by a 60mg breakthrough dose. With virtually no MAO left in the body, this breakthrough dose will catapult the explorer into the most incredible DMT experience available to humanity.

Micro dosing DMT is a very simple process, and it all takes place in a single hour. The important thing to understand is that the explorer must always have a small amount of DMT vapour in their lungs for the full hour. There will be approximately 200 breaths taken in one hour. Each inhale begins the same way. With lungs emptied, the explorer sucks into their mouth a small amount of DMT vapour... no more than a mouthful. The remaining space in the lungs is then filled with fresh room air by chasing the mouthful of vapour with a full, deep inhale. Each of the 200 inhales starts with a mouthful of vapour and is topped up with a full inhale of room air. Hit, top off, and hold.

The purpose of MdDMT is to gradually use up the body's supply of *Monoamine Oxidase*. Once that hour has been completed, it is time to initiate the psychedelic experience. This is done by inhaling a large breakthrough dose of DMT. With very little MAO present in the body, this breakthrough dose will result in the perfect experience every time.

I think I have covered the basics of micro dosing DMT.

CHAPTER 3 - MY SAFETY

As with any psychedelic adventure, safety must be your primary concern.

The first time you micro dose DMT, it is HIGHLY recommended you do it in the privacy of your own home. You should never micro dose DMT at a party. This is an experience between you and your Creator. It is a very personal, private, and spiritual occasion.

Micro dosing DMT produces a 'trip' that lasts 25 minutes. If you add that to the length of time needed to do the micro dosing step, the entire process lasts only 85 minutes. That's 60 minutes of MdDMT followed by the 25 minute psychedelic trip. You only need to find a couple hours of free time in order to do it all, start to finish.

Make sure your windows and doors are closed and locked. Ensure that balconies are locked. Create a safe environment for yourself. Explorers must ensure that their surroundings are 'trip safe'. You cannot skip this step.

Treat this experience as you would any other psychedelic experience. It is your own safety that you need to ensure.

As with any psychedelic, having a trusted trip sitter accompany you is a great idea. You may choose to have assistance during the 'micro dosing hour', thus reducing the workload of weighing, loading, or watching the clock. Once the psychedelic portion of the trip starts, you can easily ask your assistant to remain with you, or exit to another adjacent room until your trip is over.

The time of day is also important. You need to choose a time when you are least likely to be disturbed by phone calls and door knocks. You don't want any unexpected visitors or interruptions.

The clothing you wear is quite important. The wrong thing can be a nuisance later. Avoid jeans, jackets, turtlenecks, buttons, zippers, pockets, and shoes. Tight clothing is a definite no. Dress as if you will be lying on a hot beach. MdDMT will cause the explorer to feel very warm, not unpleasantly warm, but very warm, so dress very lightly. A t-shirt and loose shorts, a nightgown, bathing suit, or simply just underwear, are great choices. Many people choose to wear nothing when doing psychedelics.

Do not eat any food in the 2 hours prior to micro dosing. You MUST have an empty stomach, or you will vomit. I really mean that. Do not drink alcohol or take other drugs prior to micro dosing DMT. Respect the process and take the trip sober.

Individuals who are on prescription medication should research the possible interactions that may occur when mixing DMT and their medication. Although we are not using an actual MAOi to extend the trip, this experience certainly involves one's serotonin receptors. I recommend discussing your specific situation with your doctor before making your decision.

Finally, you should plan on recording your experience. Having a video to watch later will greatly enhance your ability to remember the trip.

CHAPTER 4 - MY METHOD

It is now time to micro dose some DMT.

The four items we need are 500mg DMT, the vaporizer (with 2 bowls), an accurate digital scale, and some inert marijuana (or similar) to act as a bed for the DMT to sit on. We also need a clock, which I assume everyone will have.

Over the next couple of hours, this will be your last chance to go to the bathroom. You really should take care of that now.

The first step is to decide where you want to do it. In my home, my choices were a couch in the living room, or my bed. I chose to do it in my bedroom because that made it easier to keep my cats away for a few hours. Pets, like phone calls, are temporarily unwelcome. I cleared off the night table beside my bed, and placed the vaporizer, with bowl and whip, within my left arm's reach. Once setup, I plugged it in and turned it on, setting the temperature to 180°F or 83°C, then let it warm up for several minutes.

Now, let's prepare the first bowl. As you can see, there is a screen located at the bottom of the glass bowl. This is where you will place the layer of pre-vaped marijuana, as a bed for the DMT to sit on. The thickness of this bottom layer should be no less than .5" (12 mm).

With the bedding material now in place, weigh out 200mg (.2 grams) of DMT powder and carefully add it on top of the bed.

The final step in preparing the bowl is to sandwich the DMT between an additional layer of bedding material (pre-vaped and crumbled marijuana). This should almost fill the vaporizer bowl. Do not pack it down as packing will impede air flow later.

With the bowl properly packed, place it on top of the vaporizer. The final step in bowl preparation is topping it off with the whip hose. Connect the correct end of the whip to the vaporizer and ensure that it fits snugly on top of the prepped bowl.

With the "hit, top off, and hold" bowl packed, and the whip attached, the micro dosing stage is ready to go.

But wait! We must weigh up the final dose that is needed to initiate "the trip". Once you have completed the micro dosing phase, you will need to have 60mg of DMT weighed up and ready to vaporize. You don't want to be weighing anything after you begin, so make sure it is all done now.

Using the second bowl, prepare it in the exact same manner. Lay the bedding material in place on the screen.

Weigh up 60mg and add this to the bowl, on top to the bed. Finally, sandwich it in the middle by adding the inert topping. This is the "initiating bowl". Place this loaded bowl beside the vaporizer, ready and waiting for use at the end of the hour of micro dosing.

From here on in, let me take you along for the adventure. I promise you; it is about to get wild.

I situate myself comfortably on my bed, propped up by pillows against the headboard. My vaporizer is warmed up and ready to go. I pick up the whip and take a few puffs on the mouthpiece. I do it as if I'm lighting a cigar... puff, puff, puff. I stare at the hose to see when vapour appears in it. I don't want to inhale any vapour; I am simply priming the hose... drawing vapour up into it. These first few wasted puffs will draw heat up through the bowl and carry vapour into the whip. As soon as I see that I have vapour coming out of the mouthpiece on the whip, it's time to begin.

This is micro dosing DMT.

I check my watch. It is midnight, or 0000 hrs.

I pick up the whip and hold the mouthpiece in my left hand.

I exhale all the air in my lungs.

I place my lips on the mouthpiece.

I draw a mouthful of vapour into my mouth.

I take only a mouthful, and no more.

With this vapour in my mouth, I remove my lips from the whip and continue to inhale fresh, room air to complete the inhale.

Lungs full of mostly room air and a little DMT, I count to 10 silently in my head.

I then exhale completely and repeat the process of inhaling a mouthful of DMT, topped off with room air.

After every inhale, I count to 10 before exhaling

Following this method, it works out to be about 3 inhale/hold/exhale cycles every 55 seconds. In an hour, that works out to 200 inhalations. Interestingly, I started with 200mg of DMT. This method of micro dosing gives me a dosage of about 1 milligram per inhale.

It is a very simple, yet repetitive process. The goal is to always have a small amount of DMT in the lungs. This is what will gradually reduce the body's available MAO. This very process acts as a monoamine oxidase inhibitor (MAOi). Maintaining a relaxed and consistent inhalation schedule is absolutely critical.

I check my clock. It is 12:10 am, or 0010 hrs. I feel totally normal. There is very little taste to the DMT when consumed in these micro doses. It is also very smooth on the lungs and doesn't burn at all. There are no signs or symptoms of anything out of the ordinary. I have successfully maintained my routine of 3 small sips each minute. It is very boring to just sit and inhale and count, but I continue.

I check my clock. It is 0020 hrs. I feel slightly drunk. In the last few minutes, I mistakenly inhaled a bit too much in one hit. I had let my mind wander and let my guard down. I stopped paying attention to the dosing cycle. There was no negative effect from this accidental 5 mg dose. I simply felt a nice rush that lasted 10 seconds and then faded away, leaving me to feel a bit inebriated. It served as a wakeup call. I have to pay attention!

Clock says 0035 hrs.

Well, I have had another couple screw ups. I did it again. I took a few sips that were too big, and now I am at that stage of drunk when I just can't shut up. I am talking to myself about useless shit. I can only talk when I exhale. I can't speak when I'm inhaling or holding my breath, so I do it on the exhale. My ability to speak clearly is gone. I am mumbling gibberish to myself. I am quite able to think clearly, but my mouth doesn't work well at all. My thinking mind is unaffected while my ability to speak is quite impaired. I am still focused on the mission at hand. Take a sip of DMT, hold it, count, and exhale. I continue.

Clock says 0040 hrs.

I am feeling great although there's still nothing happening in the psychedelic sense. I'm talking to myself, but not outwardly. I'm thinking in my head. I start a sentence and then halfway through it, I begin a new sentence on another topic. I'm not really finishing any of my thoughts... and they are very random, nothing worth mentioning. I continue with the micro dosing process.

A few minutes later, I hear a voice in my head that is not me. It is a male voice, but I'm not in control of what he is saying. He says to me, "What are you doing?" In my head, I respond with a brief, "I don't know". Again, he asks, "What are you doing?" to which I respond, "I don't know."

He continues asking me this simple question over and over again. While I continue inhaling small amounts of DMT, holding for a 10 count, and exhaling, this voice repeatedly asks me what I'm doing. My answer is always the same... I don't know. This seemingly pointless back and forth between us continues for a few minutes.

Once it becomes clear to him that I have no answer to give, he changes the question. Now the question becomes, "What do you want to do?" Another question that I don't have an answer for.

Why is there a voice in my head talking to me? Who is this voice? I have my own questions right now, and the truth is I have no idea what I'm doing. Inhaling, holding, and exhaling. The question of what I want to do seems impossible to answer.

This mystery voice continues asking the same question. "What do you want to do?" My answers to him are again a lazy, "I don't know". For several minutes this questioning continues. There seems to be nothing else he wants to ask me.

Clock says 0047 hrs.

I have been sipping DMT for 47 minutes. In the last few minutes, I have said the words 'I don't know', no less than 20 times, to this unidentified man inside my head.

He continues to ask me what I want to do; over and over. Eventually, I truly consider his question. What *do* I want to do?

As I exhale, he asks, "What do you want to do?" Now, looking for his advice, I respond by asking him, "What can I do?"

He replies, "You can do anything. What do you want to do?" My response is simple, "I want my place to be like a Star Trek holo-deck. I want to see whatever I want to see, right here in my apartment."

Now he becomes louder and more forceful, but not scary or aggressive. He sounds excited for me. It seems he has heard an answer that he can work with. He responds to my desire of having my own personal private holo-deck with, "Yes! You can do that! But you must smoke more!"

I continue sipping the DMT and I consider what he just said. I can do it, but I must smoke more. I like the first half of that, but I don't really want to do more. I feel good right now. I like how I feel. I'm drunk and feeling great. Maybe this is why people enjoy DMT... a mellow buzz. Everything seems great just as it is.

I tell him, "I don't want to smoke more." He says, "You have to smoke more if you want it to happen."

I say, "No. I'm not ready", and continue with my inhales and exhales. He repeatedly insists that I must do more if I want anything to happen. I respond every time with, "No, I'm not ready".

A few minutes pass with this back and forth between us.

"If you want anything to happen, you need to smoke more. Are you ready?" he asks me, again and again, probably 10 times. My answer is always negative.

Finally, very loudly and sternly, he says to me. "If you want anything to happen, you're going to have to smoke more. You need to smoke more."

With that, something has changed. Rather than feeling scared to 'do more', now I feel the complete opposite. Now I really want to smoke more. In just a few seconds, I've experienced a complete, 180-degree turnaround. I'm now the opposite of scared. I am excited!

Clock says 0056 hrs.

The micro dosing phase has now concluded. I've slowly ingested 200mg of DMT over 56 minutes. I have very little MAO in my system. I am no longer frightened. It is time to initiate the trip.

I look to my left and see my table and vaporizer. I still have the whip in my left hand. I know I need to swap the used bowl (that started with 200mg) out and replace it with my unused second bowl that contains the 60mg *Initiating Dose*. I also feel drunk and don't have perfect control of my arms and hands. I realize I must sit up and use both hands to accomplish the bowl swap.

So, I clumsily sit up and hang my legs off the left side of my bed. Now I can reach the vaporizer with both hands. I use my right hand to remove the whip from the bowl. I use my left hand to remove the used-up first bowl from the vaporizer and I place it on the table. I quickly, with the same hand, pick up the second bowl, the *Initiating Dose*, and place it on top of the vaporizer. The final step is fitting the whip back on top of the Initiating bowl. This process of swapping the bowls may sound difficult to do, but it only takes about 10 or 15 seconds time. **Most importantly, do not burn your fingertips on the hot glass bowl or whip fitting. Do your best to handle these by not touching glass. It will be very hot.**

With the bowls swapped, I reposition myself on my bed, propped up by pillows against my headboard. I check my watch as I begin inhaling the first Initiating hit. I breathe in a deep, long, full hit from the whip.

Clock says 0058 hrs.

With my lungs full of pure DMT vapour, I begin counting to ten.   At least, I try to count, but there's something happening.

There is a party in my lungs. It's a celebration! I have fireworks going off inside my lungs. I am hearing hundreds of voices, coming from my lungs, shouting with great joy! Within my chest, there is a massive fourth of July or New

Years Eve party happening! It can't be possible, but it's happening! I hear many voices screaming to me "Thank you, thank you! We've waited so long! Thank you!"

It's impossible to explain how mind blowing this is. I've never had anything like this happen. I'm not even counting to 10. I'm looking down at my chest to witness the fireworks. The inside of my chest is quite literally filled with… saturated with the best computer-generated graphics Hollywood can produce! I feel like every cell in my lungs is an actual, individual, life form, and they are each yelling to me "Thank You!" The celebration continues with millions of individuals thanking me. My own lungs are thanking me. How can this be?

I finally exhale that first hit, and quickly take a huge second. The festivities swell up again. They say "Thank you so much! We've waited forever for this! We never thought it would happen! Thank you. Thank you!"

I exhale that second hit. I take a huge third hit and begin holding it. The lung party is ending. I sense that there is work to be done by the partiers. The celebration is over. I begin to exhale my last hit…

CHAPTER 5 - ME

As I begin to exhale that dose, I immediately know that I don't need another hit. As I finish exhaling, I hear a female voice coming from in front of me and up to my left, from above me. Her voice is clear, and huge, and makes my bedroom sound like a movie theatre. She says three simple words, "Don't be scared."

In just seconds, those three kind words do the following. I am sober, 100% sober. My drunken state is completely gone. This is nice. It happened in the blink of an eye.

More impressively, those words completely disconnected my fear circuitry. While there may be many reasons that she said those words to me, I am absolutely certain that from this point on, I will experience no fear at all. None. I am aware of a disconnection or disabling of my fear circuitry. In seconds, I've realized I am in no danger whatsoever. There is a woman, an entity from here that cares for my happiness and safety. Her words hit me like a giant, loving hug. With her on my side, I'm not scared of ANYTHING.

All there is to do now for me is relax. I check the time.

Clock says 0100 hrs.

I look around and see my bedroom furniture buried under dirty laundry. My acoustic guitar sits on a stand. Nothing's happening. I'm totally sober but definitely excited after hearing that woman's voice. I assume something is going to happen to me at some point and I wait. And I wait. All is quiet and still in my bedroom. I blankly stare at the wall facing me, in front of me.

I begin to see rectangular blocks coming towards my forehead. They are originating from beyond my bedroom wall. These blocks appear to be identical to one another. As I examine them, I see that they are cases... the kind that you can store stuff in. They have rounded corners, re-enforced edges, and handles on top. There are many of them. Each one looks very much like a well made flight case. These cases are flying in from a distance beyond my wall. It looks amazing. Each case is outlined by a golden glow.

Each case begins slowing down as it approaches my forehead, and then finally 'lands' inside my head. With each landing, I feel a distinct click in my head. I can feel each case seat itself into a base or receptacle that lies just behind my forehead.

At first, the cases are arriving at a rate of maybe seven per second, and they sound like popcorn popping, but eventually, their number decreases until there are just a handful incoming. Then, the last case clicks into place. A solid, definitive, final click.

With that big click, I begin thinking about everything that has happened. I remember the lung party, and the woman that said, "Don't be scared". And now I've had these boxes fly in from another dimension or something. This is very bizarre, but not at all frightening. It's exciting.

There doesn't seem to be anything happening right now, but I'm hoping something starts.

Suddenly, all I can see is black, total blackness. I don't know if my eyes are open or closed.

Oh! There is a flash of light and I recognize that a match has just been struck and now burns right in front of me. The glow illuminates a white rope hanging at an arm's length away. The rope comes down from above and the end dangles in the center of my vision. I watch as the flame moves to the rope and touches it, igniting the rope... and I realize this isn't rope. This is a fuse. The type of 'rope' you find poking out of the end of a stick of dynamite. I'm intrigued.

As the fuse burns, it looks exactly, and I mean exactly, like a child's sparkler from a fireworks vendor. There are yellowy-white sparks flying in all directions. I watch it burn for a few seconds, and then my normal vision returns.

I look around my room, and ask out loud, "What the fuck just happened?"

Everything seems normal, but what the hell was the fuse business all about? I check the clock.

Clock says 0101 hrs.

It's only been a single minute since I last checked the time.

I know something's going to happen. Something is happening. I feel myself... going up, rising. I'm not actually lifting off my bed, but I feel like I am going up. I feel like I am going up in an elevator, ascending.

Something else has now started and I can't believe it.

I can feel a spot between my legs that is only the size of a grain of sand, and yet it is producing the most incredible sensation I have ever felt in my life. The feeling is instantly recognizable. This is an orgasm. Specifically, this is peak orgasm. I don't mean it's similar to peak orgasm. I truly mean it is peak orgasm. This is the 'flash' of peak orgasm. That one second of bliss.

I can't believe what's happening. It's only been four seconds, and I have already experienced the longest orgasmic flash of my life, and it's not stopping. It can't be possible. At this point, a mere five seconds of this, and I have an instant erection. In fact, I think it took about 3 seconds to become fully erect.

A few more seconds into the trip and the size of the orgasm has already grown from that of a grain of sand, to that of a grape. As its size increases, so does the bliss it produces. I look at my watch.

Clock says 0101 hrs.

I feel like I'm stuck at peak orgasm, constant, unending, and growing. I question out loud, "Is this it? Is this the trip?" There's nothing happening except for pure bliss and the sensation of lifting upward.

Tears of joy are streaming down my face. This is a dream come true. I simply lay there in my room, looking at the walls, with an erection, experiencing constantly increasing peak orgasm.

A few minutes ago, I was terrified to do a drug, and now I'm the happiest person on Earth.

This is the dream of not only every psychonaut, but it's the dream of every human being. I sit there and enjoy it as anyone would.

I'm mesmerized by this small nuclear reactor of orgasmic bliss that continues to grow within my pelvis. I can look down at my body and see this circle of bliss within my pelvis. It glows brightly with a yellow/white light. The bliss is contained within the circle. My arms and head and chest feel no bliss. Only the part of my body that is in this ever-enlarging circle feels the bliss. As the circle expands, so does the bliss it produces.

Some amount of time passes.

I start thinking about everything that is happening. Does this happen for everybody? Why have I never heard of this? How is this possible? What did I do to have this? How is it that no one ever talks about this?

Clearly, other people have done this too. I'm not the only one. Who was the woman that spoke to me at the beginning of all this? She knew something was going to happen to me and that's why she said, "Don't be scared." Hmmm. She knew this would happen to me.

But does this happen to everyone that does whatever I did? I consider the options. Maybe this happens to me, but everyone else gets a different experience. Can I really be the only person that gets 'this' trip? It must happen to everyone. I'm not unique, I'm a normal human. Everybody loves orgasmic bliss... not just me.

Whatever is happening to me right now, will happen for anyone that does whatever I did.

I've been here for a while now, and I understand that I will never die. I know my body will die, but my soul, the 'thing' that sits between my ears, and looks out my eyes, never dies. I realize the woman at the beginning is from this side of reality. She's not a human. She's an entity of immense importance and status. I understand that she greets EVERYBODY when they arrive here. She is here for every single human being. She welcomes each of us when we arrive here.

How have I never heard of any of this? If this happens to me, it must happen to everyone. We are all humans. I understand now that we are all built the same. On the outside, we are very different. On the inside, we are identical. We all have a soul. I'm sure that whatever I am doing right now will happen to everyone that does it. I am not rare.

The bliss is continuing to grow. I lose interest in thinking about anything. I stare at my penis and simply enjoy 'the trip'. I think of nothing, my mind is blank.

After what seems to be several hours, I open my eyes and I'm immediately stunned by the orgasmic bliss that's rising in me. I seem to have forgotten about it while I was daydreaming. My room looks completely normal. I don't hear any noises in my building. Everything seems fine. I feel safe.

I look down and see a glowing ball of energy inside my abdomen. I begin thanking whoever is responsible for this. I'm not imagining this. There is a force or entity somewhere that is responsible for all this. There must be a creator or God. Humans did not create this experience... and somehow, I am doing it right now! This is something created by God, for me. I know this.

Tears are streaming down my cheeks continuously while I say thank you, thank you, over and over again. I know I'm not alone, although my room is empty of people. For the first time in my life, I realize that I am not alone... and I've never been alone. Even when alone, I was never alone. The creator of this experience has been with me every single second of my life, I just didn't know it.

Nobody taught me about this. Doesn't anybody else know about this? If this happens to me, it will happen to everybody. I understand... nobody is alone. The 'Being' responsible for all of this, is universal to all of us.

I get lost in the bliss. Imagine a never ending peak orgasm that has been multiplied by a factor of billions. I could enjoy this forever. I love staring at my penis.

Time passes.

What happens now is what I call a scene change. Out of nowhere and totally unexpectedly, I am instantly immersed in blackness. All around me is just black space. I arrive here with no thoughts or memory of what has been occurring. I don't remember my room. I don't even remember the bliss. I'm just surrounded by black space.

And then I see a line in front of me. It stretches from my far right and goes all the way to the left and beyond. Imagine a horizon line. I wonder what it is. It looks very far away. After a few seconds it starts to move closer to me. As it gets closer I recognize it as an electrical wire. Then I see energy flowing through the wire, from right to left.

I peer into this bright yellow/white flow of energy, and within it I can see many small packets. In fact, the entire stream of energy consists only of these small, brightly illuminated packets. As I inspect this energy flow, I realize that each packet contains information.

Time passes.

Every packet of information is like a book. It contains a massive amount of information about a specific topic or idea. There are billions of books in this energy stream. I am astonished by the amount of information that I am witnessing. I'm not reading any of the books. I am simply seeing that they exist. I am being shown that there is so much knowledge that I am unaware of. I understand that humans don't have access to 'these books'. I'm in a different world right now.   These books, and this knowledge, only exist here... wherever I am.

I spend a long time watching this massive amount of information flow past me. I acknowledge that my Creator is responsible for this. I understand this at my very core. No human will ever convince me that there is no Creator. I am experiencing the Creator's work right now. Again, I feel like the luckiest human on the planet. I want every person to experience this! I am watching something that cannot be believed, and yet, here I am.

I know I did something in my room earlier that caused all this to happen, but I don't remember exactly what I did. I know it was a drug and I know it was quick and easy.

In absolute darkness I continue watching the energy flow by in this electrical wire suspended in front of me.

Time passes.

I understand that death is not to be feared in any way. There is no need to be scared because we don't die. The body dies, but the thing that sits between my ears, and looks out my eyes… that thing lives forever. When I die, I simply shed my body like dirty clothing, and then I put on some clean clothes. I'm not scared of dying now. I was terrified of dying a few hours ago though. I've been terrified of death my entire adult life. I understand now that I have no reasons at all to be scared. Somehow, the world I am in right now… will be waiting for me when I die.

I don't remember how I got here. I know I did a drug, in my room, by myself. It must be a drug that other people know about. I wish I could remember how I got here. I mean, this whole trip has changed my life! This is something anyone can do. The whole world fears dying. Everyone is terrified of dying. I know this is a fact.

What has happened to me? I become ecstatic. I can see myself as a little boy, jumping up and down, and doing cartwheels in a playground. He is so happy and exploding with glee! I can see myself celebrating the most wonderful realization ever. That little boy realizes death is a lie.

And that little boy is me!

That happy little boy will live a life free of fear from this moment on. I will never fear death again. I'm never, ever, alone. I start crying because realizing I am bullet-proof truly means I will live forever, under the care of my Creator. I feel like I have 'cured death'. I am so proud of myself for doing… whatever I did to get to here.

Time passes.

I wonder what I did. I wonder how long I've been doing this. It feels like a long time. Time seems pretty weird here. This trip must end sometime. It seems like I've been doing this for hours. It feels like days. This has got to end sometime.

Time passes.

I remember that some time ago, I was concerned about a clock. The time was important to me earlier. I wonder what that was all about. I hope there wasn't a reason for the clock.

Oh shit! I work later!

My eyes pop open wide! I am immediately enveloped by orgasmic bliss beyond imagination! Oh my God, I forgot about this! Simultaneously, I remember my job at 1000 hrs. I turn and look at my clock, expecting to see a time that ensures I've lost my job.

Clock says 0103 hrs.

Now, somewhere in me, there is a sober me. A smart me. I can do math in my head. I look at that time and I just can't believe it. I remember what I'm doing. I'm smoking DMT. My trip started at... 0100 hrs... and it has been only 3 minutes since I started. I feel like it has been 8 hours at least... or perhaps even days. I have no idea how it's only been 3 minutes.

My eyes fly open, and I'm immediately brought back to my physical reality of peak orgasm. It hits me like a baseball bat to the face. I had completely forgotten about it again. Instantly, I return to being the happiest human on Earth. I take a slow motion look at my clock.

Clock says 0103 hrs.

I sit in orgasmic and spiritual bliss. I allow myself to forget about time. I soak up the bliss like a sponge.

I get lost in my own thoughts.

I stare at my penis and think this must end soon. This trip must be over soon. I've been doing this forever! It must end. It can't go on forever... but it seems like it is. It must be over soon.

I've already figured everything out. I got the whole spiritual experience. I know there's a power bigger than me... and it created me... and I'll never die. OK. I get it.

I'm still floating up. That feeling of 'going up' hasn't stopped. I feel like I'm on an elevator.

Time passes.

I notice how my skin feels to me. It feels hot! It's just like laying on a super hot beach in the sun, but I'm not sweating at all. It feels very nice. It feels like a yummy hot blanket all over me.

So, are we done yet? Or is this 'it'? This is... everything... right? We must be getting close to the end of this. What else is there?

In an instant, I'm somewhere else. I'm surrounded by black space. Far away, in front of me there is a line that stretches from right to left. I can't see what it is, but it begins to move closer to me. I recognize it as a garden hose, a typical backyard garden hose. It continues to move closer and closer to my eyes until it stops at about an arm's length away. It is now a 12 inch thick garden hose, right in front of me.

As I look at the hose, I begin to see inside of it. I can see water flowing from right to left. It appears to be a very strong flow of lots of water. No, it's not water. It's yellow and white energy... and very bright. I see information passing by. I wonder what I'm seeing.

Scene change! I am standing in a library, a very huge library. There are multiple floors with shelves of books. This is an old library with no computers. I see endless rows of dusty books, all arranged by categories. There are sections for different topics. I think how much this would have blown my mom's mind. She loved books so much! How can there be a library this big? This is just massive. Nobody else is here, I'm all by myself. Am I supposed to go look at these books?

I don't see a librarian. There's no one here to help me pick out a book. Who's in charge here? What is this place?

Scene change! I am staring at a huge garden hose that is laid out right in front of my face. Energy is surging through it with great, unearthly force. This is pressure that can cut steel. Look at that energy. Wow!

The garden hose begins to rotate and turn its left end towards my face. I don't know what to expect, but I am not scared at all. I await the blast. Sure enough, this energy finds my face and starts blasting me. I don't feel any pain. This energy is flowing through my face and exiting out the back of my head. Information that I have never seen before is now penetrating my head at an unbelievable rate. I quickly understand that the Librarian has granted my wish... and now I am being force fed every book in that library. She started with book number one and jammed that through me. Then she shoved book number two through my head. Then I realize these books are all about me. The entire library is about me, and nobody else. Upon that realization, the pace really picks up.

I am staring straight at energy as it bombards my face. I love it. Information is entering me in a perfectly, pre-planned, specific order. I'm not choosing the books. My Librarian Lady is doing all the work. It seems the contents of one book lead to the contents of the next book. Every book prepares you for the next book. These are like steps. They are taken in a specific order. These books are going through me faster than any computer could ever keep up with.

It seems impossible. I have millions of books, all about me, flowing through me right now. Not one other person is even mentioned in any of the books. I am the subject of all of it. I fucking love this, I really do.

Time passes while I read.

I wonder. If I wanted to describe this whole 'energy blast of books' to other people… what would I say? How would I describe this?

Time passes as I multi-task. I think and read.

I guess I would say the energy is like wind, and I am like the screen of a window. The wind blows through me, and I get it all. I understand the wind as it blows through me. These books blow through me like wind though a screen.

I continue digesting one book after another.

Eventually, I remember that I work later. I need to check the clock…

I open my eyes and WHAM! I'm smashed with orgasmic bliss beyond possibility. Oh my God it's still happening!

I just soak up the bliss.

I think about what just happened… the library and water hose. It's unbelievable. It's impossible. But it also just happened. I didn't imagine that. I could never imagine that. It really happened.

I begin thanking someone again. I don't know who is responsible for all this, but I just keep saying thank you over and over again to the air in the room. Someone is doing all of this for me. I love them so much.

I suddenly realize what just happened. All those books I just read were my blueprint! I have a spiritual blueprint! I am real! I am a literal structure of some sort. I'm not just an invisible fart in the cosmic wind... I fucking exist! I have a building that is me! I understand now that I exist beyond the normal 3D world. I'm a soul. I am a soul.

There is a little boy inside of me dancing around with his arms in the air. He is experiencing pure, childish joy! He's the happiest little boy ever.

I wonder when this is going to end. It seems to be going on for a long time. What was the time last time I checked? I don't remember. It feels like I haven't checked the time for a while. Look at that little boy having fun. He's so thrilled!

Shit! I need to check the clock. Eyes fly open and...

Clock says 0104 hrs.

Now come on... how can that be? What the fuck is going on here? It's only been 4 fucking minutes since I started this? What's wrong with time?

I still feel myself going up in an elevator. Time is screwed up.

I can feel a new sensation. It's a body buzz... a strong buzz... maybe a vibration. I love it.

The orgasmic bliss is so blinding that I can feel it tugging at the corners of my eyes. I glance down at my penis and see a fiery ball of energy glowing inside of me. I start to stare at myself again.

Time passes.

I am surrounded by just the blackness of space. I wonder what just happened. Directly in front of me is a huge, giant river that flows from right to left. There is yellow/white energy flowing through the river. The energy churns and bubbles. The river is very wide. It's Niagara Falls wide. I can not only hear the rumble of the energy flowing, but I can feel it too. I can feel the power of the flow. It feels like a constant earthquake.

Once I recognize that it's a river of energy, it immediately turns in my direction and the energy starts going through me. This massive river of energy blasting through every cell of my body does not hurt at all. It feels wonderful to literally absorb information from another dimension or world or wherever I am. Volumes of data, all about me, punch through my human body.

It's intense, but simple. This is more of my blueprint! It's all about me.

I remember the first blueprint... that was my structure... a brick building. Now, this new blueprint has to do with my wiring, my plumbing. This blueprint goes deeper than the first one.

I realize to an even greater extent than before, I am real! I understand how I exist and what I am at the core.

I'm truly learning that I am truly a real, literal soul. I'm being shown my internal mechanisms and processes. I am real, and I have content.

While the little boy in my head celebrates with cartwheels and handstands, I bask in the information that is me... my own personal soul-blueprint.

This is so real... and no one will ever believe it. I'm living the dream right now. This is fucking magic, for real! I'm so excited!

This knowledge squeezes past my molecules and I absorb it all. A river of information, all about me, flows through me. What is happening to me?

What is going on here? Why is all this happening?

What the hell am I doing? It was a little while ago that I started doing something in my bedroom... and now this is happening.

What's going on?

And then, I feel a bit annoyed that I'm not getting an answer to my simple question. It's a simple question. I'd like an answer.

And then I remember my manners. I remember that I'm not alone. There is someone or something responsible for ALL of this. I've been thanking them all day and I know they exist. I decide to ask nicely, for the first time.

I say out loud and clear, "Please tell me what's happening to me. I don't know what's going on right now... and I would really like to know. Please tell me."

I immediately get a response from above, to my front, left corner. She says "This is Kundalini"

Oh my God, there she is! I knew she was with me!

I consider her answer. WOW! I've heard of that! I can't believe she said that. I've heard of that before. My mom had a book on her shelf when I was a kid. It was called Kundalini Rising. I would ask her what Kundalini meant, and she would give me some confusing answer. I never figured it out. But I know now that I can look it up when this trip is over. That makes me so happy to finally have a word that humans have heard before... a word that I can call this whole thing that is happening to me.

I continue to allow the blissful river of knowledge to drill its way through my body. I think about Kundalini. I wonder what that's all about. I better not forget what she called it. Fuck, that would really suck hard if I forget what she said. Aaron, buddy... don't forget what she said, or you'll be mad later. You'll be really pissed with yourself. Don't fuckin' forget this buddy. You have a memory like a fuckin' sieve. You gotta remember this shit. Pay attention.

Time passes.

Now I'm thinking about clocks. I wonder why. Why am I concerned with time? It seems like I've been concerned about time for a long time. Hmm. This all seems to be lasting for a long time.

Hey Buddy. Do you think this is the trip? I think I do. What if it isn't? What if you are just imagining all this? What about that?

When is this going to end?

My eyes open slowly, very slowly. I remember what's happening this time. I know I'm about to be absolutely obliterated by peak orgasm bliss… and I'm ready for it.

My body is still vibrating from the big river! Every cell seems to be humming. I can feel a wind blowing on my face. I look around my room and nothing is happening. I look down at my fat belly and see the big nuclear glowing ball of bliss has grown larger. It has expanded and it's up to where my belly button is located. Within this magical ball of energy, I see my happy penis.

I feel like I'm sitting in a storm of some sort. My room is rumbling, I'm buzzing. There's a strong wind in my face. My body feels very warm, my skin is hot.

I am so beyond happy, it's crazy. This is just nuts. Who would believe this?

The wind and rumbling in my room become more intense with every second. I wonder if the whole World feels this. I wonder how long I've been doing this.

In slow motion I slowly turn my head to the left, and there's my clock.

Clock says 0109 hrs.

The wind is increasing. I do the math. I started doing this…
whatever… 9 minutes ago. Is that right? Tell me… is that
right?

There's so much wind in my face right now, I can barely
keep my eyes open. It sounds and feels like a train is
passing my bedroom. It's loud and windy and everything is
shaking. I'm not scared, but I am certainly curious.

The orgasmic bliss is continuing to grow. That circle in me
is getting bigger. Everything is increasing.

I can't keep my eyes open, and I close them.

Directly in front of my face, six inches away from my nose,
is literally, Niagara Falls. Imagine Niagara Falls. It's huge…
a wonder of the world. Now, change the watercolor from
blue to gold. Now, you need to scale it down so that it is
only one foot wide. Finally, place it right in front of your
face. Now you have a small golden waterfall, right in front
of your face.

It's right there. I can feel the water mist hitting my face. I
feel the wind created by the water falling past my face. I
hear the rumbling… the undeniable power of it.

I lean forward, placing my face right in it. I bury my face in
this golden waterfall. Time stops. This is bliss beyond bliss.

I lean back a little to remove myself from the waterfall. Did
that really happen?

I simply do it again. I don't even have to move my body. I just think 'lean forward'.

I bathe in energy. There is no time. There is nothing but love. There is just love. There is a specific someone that is showing me that there is only love. There is nothing but love. Everything else is illusion. I want to stay here forever.

Eventually I decide to pull my head out of Niagara Falls. I see it right in front of me. I lean back in. Why not?

There comes a time in the waterfall when I wonder what is happening. At some point I remember that I'm not alone.

I blurt out the words, "What is happening now? Please tell me."

She responds with three words, "This is Ankh."

Again, I am thrilled to hear her speak. I say thank you to her many times.

I stay in there for a long time before emerging from the bliss. It's all love, and nothing else. There is nothing other than love. I fucking get that now. It makes so much sense.

But what is this waterfall? Am I the only person that knows about this? The whole world needs to know about this!

Nobody would believe me. I will have to research Ankh when this is all done and over with.

Visually, my room looks normal. However, to me, it feels like a hurricane is happening right in front of me.

I look down at my body. The circle of bliss has made it all the way to my neck! My room seems like it will explode. I feel myself rising in that elevator.

Will this ever end? I look at my clock.

Clock says 0115 hrs.

I am so overwhelmed by everything that's happening. I simply sit and do nothing.

Suddenly, out of nowhere, there is a popping sound. Like a cartoon bubble popping. One pop, and the top of my head flies open. Pop! From top to bottom, side to side, and front to back; my mind instantly fills the Universe.

I feel like I am everywhere all at the same time. My consciousness now literally fills the Universe. I am everywhere, while I sit here on my bed.

Everything keeps increasing. The volume is being turned up on everything. My room looks normal, but I sure don't feel normal. I'm vibrating. I'm rising. I feel like I'm somewhere else. Orgasmic bliss is building more and more.

I hear what sounds like a hand crank air siren... winding up... getting louder and rising in pitch. There's a lot of wind blowing on my face. Everything is rumbling.

Suddenly I see a few sparks fly by my face. It looks like someone kicked the coals of a fire, and sparks flew off it. After a handful of sparks blow by me, I start seeing silver pieces of Christmas tinsel, flying towards me, from beyond my bedroom wall.

At first there was only one lone piece of silver tinsel, but quickly, there are many. At any time, there are at least twenty incoming strips of silver foil in my view. They do not penetrate me. They all seem to go around me.

The vibrations... the noise... the energy in my room is so paranormal right now. It feels like a scene from the movie Poltergeist... all the toys flying around in the kid's bedroom. My room feels like a hurricane.

Now I see both green and red strips of foil along with the silver foil strips. All three colors of tinsel are flying past me.

I can still see my wall, but only barely. My vision is almost completely blocked by all the shiny tinsel coming at me.

I know I'm lying on my bed, but I feel like I'm standing on top of a mountain peak, with my arms stretched up toward the sky. I can feel wind blowing up from below me.

I feel powerful.

Suddenly, all the foil pieces gather in the center of my vision. They create a colourful circular pattern. This pattern twitches somewhat, and then stabilizes.

It appears to be an extremely detailed flower. There are many tiny lights… thousands of bright, sharp, LED lights. It's a top view of a flower. I can see the symmetry in the petals.

I quickly recognize this flower as something that is mine. I also realize all is quiet now.

The loud noise is gone. The wind has stopped. Everything seems very quiet and still.

Suddenly, I feel like a giant invisible hand has picked me up and loaded me into the chamber of a rifle.

I'm launched at high velocity!!!!

Stars are flying by me. I am travelling at warp speed, flying through space. I am just eyeballs moving at warp speed. What I'm seeing is EXACTLY what movies show as star ships 'go to warp'. White dots… stars are whizzing by me on all sides. I can't believe what is happening. I can't believe this is really happening.

I finally arrive somewhere and come to an instant stop. I go from warp speed to zero, in an instant. All motion has ceased. All is still. I think time has stopped. Directly in front of me is a large white dot on a black background. I am given only as much time as is needed, a tiny fragment of a second, to identify what I am seeing, 'Oh, the Sun', and it explodes with a big bang!

Scene change.

I open my eyes wide in shock and I'm staring straight ahead. Time doesn't exist. Orgasmic BLISS is all that I feel. Wherever I am, there is a party going on! I think I have dropped into the biggest celebration ever.

I'm sitting outside on the ground. It's nighttime, and the sky is very black. Directly in front of me is a tall obelisk. It is silver in color and appears to be wrapped with the dull side of aluminum foil facing out. This obelisk has red and blue LED lights that are blinking on and off. These lights start at the bottom of the obelisk and run all the way to the top. Their blink pattern makes the lights look like they are moving up towards the top.

There are red and blue ribbons of bright light shooting up and out from the top of the obelisk. These energy beams are being shot straight up and out into the black sky above, illuminating my surroundings with purple flashes of light. These flashes occur once every second.

I look around and see many tall obelisks in the distance, but they have no lights on them. My obelisk has lights, the others don't.   I can also see several smaller shapes scattered around the landscape.

This reminds me of Stonehenge. I feel like I'm sitting in the circle at Stonehenge.   Are we having a party at Stonehenge? Where is... anybody? I can tell that I'm at a party, but I see no other people.

This could be a surprise birthday party... and everybody is still hiding in a closet, waiting to jump out at me.

This obelisk continues to blink its red and blue lights in an upward direction. The top of the obelisk is blasting its ribbons of light into the night sky, once per second.

Everybody seems proud of me, but there's nobody here.

Everybody seems to be looking at me, but I see nobody. I feel that I am the center of attention. All the invisible eyes are on me.

I spend a long time just roasting in the orgasmic bliss that pulses through me.

It seems like I'm at my grade eight graduation. I feel like my parents are happy with me for finishing something important.

I stare straight ahead at the huge obelisk between my legs. It is fascinating!

Eventually, I begin to better understand where I am sitting.

This is a huge cemetery. It goes in all directions forever. I'm surrounded by tombstones. This would normally scare the shit right out of me. However, I experience only bliss in this cemetery.

My tombstone, my Obelisk, is the only source of light.

The entire scene pulses with the purple flash of my fireworks in this night sky. Sexual bliss surges through me with each pulse of purple light. My eyes repeatedly bulge with pleasure. I can see the purple toned endless display of tombstones stretching off in the distance.

I am experiencing no time. I feel like a throbbing nuclear reactor, expelling energy straight up to the sky.

Time passes.

I feel like I have been here forever. I love it. There is so much happiness here… but I still see nobody else. I am simply at peak bliss… forever.

And then I receive a message. You can think of it as a telegram, an email, a text, a phone call. I literally, in my mind, receive a note that says, "Congratulations, the Moon." Mentally, I receive this, and then read it to myself.

Now… this is crazy. Did I just get a message from the Moon? The fucking Moon sent me a note? What the fuck is going on?

I receive another message in my head. It says, "Great job, proud of you, Jupiter."

I'm drowning in perfect sexual bliss and getting nice messages from… planets? Honestly, this doesn't surprise me. Where I am and what I'm experiencing, is so far away from real life… anything appears to be possible.

I suppose it's nice to get a call from a President or perhaps a celebrity, but I am getting calls from planets!

"I'm so proud of you. You did it. You made it! Alpha Centauri."

My mind fills the Universe. I feel as though I am everywhere. The Universe seems so real and close to me now.

Another message arrives in my bliss soaked mind, "Congratulations on your graduation. You earned it. Andromeda."

I start thinking about what Andromeda just said. Yes! This is my graduation! I get it! Everything I just did... was school!

At some point earlier today, I did something that made all this happen. I was in school. I started with grade one and rose through the grades. I get it now. Oh my God! That was all an education... about me.

I do mental back flips and cartwheels to celebrate! I understand that I've done something that unlocked a spiritual awakening. I don't know what I did, but I know it can be done by ANYBODY.

I receive more, many more congratulations from many, many Celestial and Cosmic bodies. Hundreds and perhaps thousands of messages clog my mental inbox.

My entire world is throbbing with a purple bliss... as I sit in a cemetery, at the base of a pulsating obelisk.

The Universe loves me. I get it. I do. I fucking get it. Yep. I understand why there is nobody here. This party is attended by only me, and the Universe. There are no humans here.

After what seems to be forever, I start thinking about clocks and time. I've been here forever, and I think I might need to check a clock. I wonder how long I've been here. I don't want to ever leave. How can I tell people about this? I already know no one would believe it. I wouldn't believe it. I wonder what time it is. I can't stay here forever.

I remember that I'm not really in a cemetery, but I'm sitting on my bed, in my bedroom.

My eyes open, in slow motion. Realizations occur, in slow motion.

I can see my room. It has a slight red tint overlaying my entire field of view. It's like I'm looking through red tinted lenses. In addition to this, I see a heads-up display... like a military display of grids and lines. The lines extend off into the distance far past my real walls. It looks like the 80's video game Battle Tank... very basic line vector graphics. These lines continue outward forever in all directions creating a grid-work... a wire diagram of a floor. If I tilt my head to the left or right, the grid doesn't move with my head. It is stationary, in place. It resembles a tiled floor with only the grout lines illuminated.

Instantly, I feel the orgasmic bliss. How can I ever explain this? I am not only at peak orgasmic, non-stop bliss (times a billion) ... but I am also now experiencing literal ejaculations. My penis pulses in perfect time with the bulging of my eyes... which bulge in perfect time with the light show being emitted from the top of the silver obelisk between my legs.

I realize the bizarre situation I am in. Now I understand why I might have trouble telling people about this. How can I tell anyone that I did this?

The staggering bliss continues.

I turn and look at the clock... all in slow motion. Tick, tick, tick, tick. Frame by frame, I turn my face, surely taking several seconds for my eyes to find their target. I focus through the red bliss and my clock indicates...

Clock says 0121 hrs.

0121. I slowly say the numbers to myself. I wonder what they mean. Zero one two one.

I remember that I did something 21 minutes ago that caused all of this.

I remember that I had a Teacher and then I went to school.

There were so many steps... and so much has happened... and it all happened in 21 minutes?

And now I'm graduating?

My eyes shut and I see the Obelisk between my legs. It deserves a capital letter now. It ejaculates blue and red energy into the sky.

I begin thinking about women. I love women. I wish there was a woman here right now.

Suddenly, a change.

I am surrounded by the blackness of space. I see directly in front of me a viewing screen or television. The screen is black just as the space around me is.

And then I see ME on the viewing screen. I am naked. I am having sex with the blackness. I literally can see myself humping the blackness of space. I am the star of my own porn video. I laugh at this. I find it to be very comical.

And then everything seems to come together. The point of all of this becomes clear. There is a slight shift in something... and suddenly I realize that I am having sex with The Universe. Literally.

I am truly having sex with The Universe. This is a trillion times more realistic to me than real life itself. This is beyond simply watching the event unfold as a porn video. I am feeling it in every cell of my existence. I have climbed a mountain to get to Her. We caress and touch each other. We are each enjoying the bliss of the moment... a moment that lasts forever.

I stand alone atop the highest mountain top, and make love to Her, The Universe, forever.

My eyes open. Something is very different. Everything looks totally normal and calm. I immediately realize that I'm not rising anymore. Somebody has taken their foot off the gas pedal and we're just coasting now. The push, the acceleration of the trip, has ended. The elevator is slowing down. The orgasmic bliss is fading. My throbbing erection is deflating.

I realize the trip is ending. I remember that I was smoking DMT. I can see it sitting on the table with my vaporizer. I listen to hear if anyone is in my apartment. It sounds quiet.

I look at my clock and it says 0125 hrs.

I feel completely sober and wonderful. I hop out of my bed, throw on some shorts, and go make a sandwich because I am starving.

I sit in my living room and think about all that just happened.

Now that it's all over I remember exactly how I did it. Later, I will investigate what 'Kundalini' and 'Ankh' mean. Eventually, I will learn that this entire 25 minute experience was the event of my Chakras being activated. My Chakras opened from bottom to top, over a 25 minute period. I will also learn that the 'Ankh' occurs during the activation of the Heart Chakra.

Unlike any other psychedelic trip, these 25 minutes are repeatable. Every time I do it, I get the same trip. The Chakras open in order from bottom to top every time.

You can do this as often as you wish, although I wouldn't suggest doing it frequently. You 'could' do it every day, but you'll also lose grip on reality quickly. As with many psychedelics, it takes at least a week for the psychonaut to comprehend and absorb their experience.

There are definite changes in one's perception of what's real. I experienced paradigm shifts in personal beliefs. I have different expectations of what happens when I die now. My belief in The Universe as a real Being is rock solid. I understand that my Soul is that which sits between my ears and behind my eyes. My Soul is what does all my thinking and wanting, every day. My memories are stored in my Soul. My wants and desires are in my Soul, not my body.

My body is 'merely' an interface for the Soul to experience the five senses. It is like clothing for the Soul. When I die, I will put on new clothing.

No human being will ever convince me that death is permanent. Death of our body is certainly definite, but death of that part within each of us that thinks and looks and hears and remembers... that is impossible.

Those are bold statements to make, but I firmly stand behind them.

This experience awaits any one with the courage to try it. Use this book as a map and as a warning. Let it help you decide if micro dosing DMT is right for you.

Before we continue any further, I would like to take us back to the end of the 25 minute Kundalini experience. I want to show you a trick I learned.

Allow me to rewind a few minutes and jump right back to the end of the trip.

Let's continue from here...

CHAPTER 6 - MY GOD

My eyes open.   Something is very different.

Everything looks totally normal and calm. I immediately realize that I'm not rising anymore. Somebody has taken their foot off the gas pedal and we're just coasting now. The push, the acceleration of the trip, has ended. The elevator is slowing down. The orgasmic bliss is fading. My throbbing erection is deflating.

I realize the trip is ending. I remember that I was smoking DMT. I can see it sitting on the table with my vaporizer. I listen to hear if anyone is in my apartment. It sounds quiet.

I look at my clock and it says 0125 hrs. I decide to smoke more.

I scoop up another initiating dose of DMT, remove the whip from atop the bowl, and dump about 60mg in on top of the used, warm contents. Quickly I replace the whip. This process needs to be done quickly. I only have about 30 seconds to get more DMT in me, or this won't work.

Immediately I inhale a big hit and start holding it for 10 seconds. I blow it out. I repeat this twice. I sit back and check the clock.

Clock says 0125 hrs.

I can now feel myself rising.   I can feel peak orgasm returning.   The trip is starting all over again.   I begin ejaculating again. That is not a joke.

I can't believe this is all happening again!

Suddenly, I feel like a giant invisible hand has picked me up and loaded me into the chamber of a rifle.

I'm launched at high velocity!!!!

Stars are flying by me. I am travelling at warp speed, flying through space. I am just eyeballs moving at warp speed. White dots... stars are whizzing by me on all sides. I can't believe this is happening again.

I finally arrive somewhere and come to an instant stop. I go from warp speed to zero, in an instant. All motion has ceased. All is still. This is total tranquility. I think time has stopped. Directly in front of me is a large white dot on a black background. I am given only as much time as is needed, a tiny fragment of a second, to identify what I am seeing, 'Oh, the Sun', and it explodes with a big bang!

Scene change.

I am sitting on the side of a mountain. Below me is a floor of clouds that glows with the color of a sunset. In the distance, to my left I see a large black mountain top poking up through the glowing clouds. To my right, I see a few more, black triangles... these are shorter mountains.

The sky above is completely black. There are no stars or sources of light in this blackness. The clouds below me are the only source of light. This ocean of clouds appears to be illuminated from below... as if there is a sunset occurring below the clouds. It seems very upside down.

Far off on the horizon, dead center in my view, I see a skyline of what looks to be a city. It is very far away but I can see the shapes of several buildings. There is one very tall building located in the center of this city. I can see that it dwarfs all the other buildings. It's very easily identifiable as an obelisk.

I sit here for a while, just enjoying the beautiful view. I've never been on a mountain, above the clouds.

I wonder what I am sitting on. Am I sitting on a chair?

Now I realize that I am sitting on the lap of someone. I feel like a little boy sitting on my dad's lap. I wonder, is this is my dad?

I realize it isn't my dad. This doesn't feel like I'm on my dad's lap anymore. It feels like I'm sitting on the lap of Santa Claus. Whoever I am sitting on is... magical.

I continue to look out over the cloud floor, illuminated by a sunset underneath.

I wonder what's going on. I consider what has happened to me today. I know that I did something in my bedroom, some time ago, and now I'm sitting here on a mountain, on the lap of someone magical.

I don't have the courage to turn around to see who it is. I know who it is now. I recognize that I'm sitting on God's lap.

Why am I being allowed to experience any of this? How can it be happening? How did I manage to get here?

I sit and consider my situation. I know He's right behind me. I don't want to start anything, so I just sit silently on His lap.

I'm quite happy to just sit here.

Finally, I ask God, "Why are you showing me this?" Without hesitation He responds, "You made the trip. You had faith. You did it."

I sit still and think about what He said.

Will I remember this? What if I don't remember this? There is no way I can forget any of this. What would be the point of any of this if I forget it all? Have other people done this and then forgotten it all? Is that why I have never heard of any of this? No one can tell their story because they can't remember it?

God must know that I will tell people about this. If I remember this, I'll tell people.

It takes a little courage to break the silence. I finally ask God, "HOW can you show me this?" I emphasize the word how. He simply responds, "I can show you this because no one will ever believe you."

Now I understand the problem. Nobody will ever believe me. I wouldn't believe it either. I've spent a lifetime of thinking those who 'meet God' are fucking crazy.

I understand how this secret is a secret that keeps itself. I don't want people to think I'm nuts, so I will never tell anyone. I wonder how many people before me have done this.

I ask God, "How many people have done this before me?"

God says nothing.

I ask, "A million?"

He says, "Lower."
"A hundred thousand?"
"Lower"
"Fifty thousand?"
"Lower"

I feel myself moving backwards. I'm moving closer to God's chest.
"Ten thousand?"
"Lower"
"One thousand???"
"Lower"

I am getting anxious. This number is coming down to an area that is making me uncomfortable. I'm getting a bit freaked out.

I continue to feel myself receding into Him.
"Five hundred?"
"Lower"

"One hundred?" I begin to feel swirly and fuzzy. My back is melting into His chest and belly.
"Lower"
I nervously ask, "Ten people?"

I can't believe what is happening. I am merging with the individual whose lap I am sitting on. Visually, everything now looks fuzzy... all dots... it feels warm and very fuzzy. I feel like I am dissolving into God. As I fall backwards in slow motion, merging with God, I hear the words echo behind me...

"It's always BEEN you you you you you"

Scene change.

I find myself standing in the foyer of a large home. In front of me there is a staircase rising to the second floor. The walls around me appear to be grey stone. There is an abundance of dark wood. There are red tapestries on the walls. The floors are marble. It looks like an old castle, with modern lighting. LED bulbs, with no shades, that cast odd, twitchy shadows on everything.

I seem to be the only person here, so I wander about and look around.

There is a display stand in the foyer, with a globe sitting on it. Imagine a globe of the Earth, from your public school years. I approach this globe and examine it.

It isn't Earth, but it is a planet. It isn't a planet from our solar system. It measures about two feet in diameter, and it rotates while suspended above the display base.

As I examine it, I realize it's alive with life. There are billions of life forms on this little ball on the table. I don't dare touch it.

I look around and find other displays in other rooms. These displays are also showcasing miniature versions of Celestial or Cosmic bodies... and they are all alive somehow.

I see on the wall, there is a large, framed poster of a black hole that is perpetually devouring itself.

I explore the castle for some time, going from one display to the next, when I realize that this is God's home! I can't believe this is happening.

As time goes on, I start to understand that everything I'm looking at... is mine. I recognize the Cosmic displays... the Celestial artwork. These are mine! I decorated this place myself!

Suddenly, I am standing in my castle, surrounded by my collection of rare Galactic art. This is my home, and it always has been. I am home.

As I begin to open my eyes, I hear the words, "Now, go explore." My eyes pop open!

I am immediately reminded of the peak orgasm bliss. My room looks totally normal. My penis is ejaculating once per second. I can't believe this is still happening.

I realize that I'm not rising anymore. Someone has taken their foot off the gas pedal and I'm coasting again. The acceleration of the trip has ended. The orgasmic bliss is slowly fading.

I realize the trip is ending. I remember that I was smoking DMT. I can see it sitting on the table with my vaporizer. I listen to hear if anyone is in my apartment. It sounds quiet. I look at my clock.

Clock says 0149 hrs.

OK. I have time and the apartment sounds quiet. Let's do it Buddy!

I scoop up another initiating dose of DMT, remove the whip from atop the bowl, and dump about 60mg in on top of the used, warm contents. I replace the whip. This process needs to be done quickly. I only have about 30 seconds to get more DMT in me, or this won't work.

Immediately I inhale a big hit and start holding it for 10 seconds. I blow it out. I repeat this twice. I sit back and check the clock.

CHAPTER 7 - MY WORLD

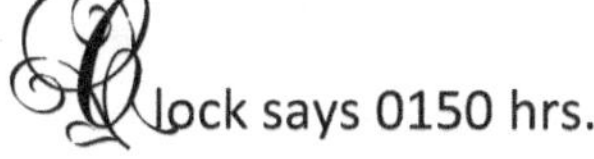

lock says 0150 hrs.

I can now feel myself rising. I can feel peak orgasm returning. The trip is starting all over again. I begin ejaculating again.

I can't believe it.

Suddenly, I feel like a giant invisible hand has picked me up and loaded me into the chamber of a rifle.

I'm launched at high velocity!!!!

Stars are flying by me. I am travelling at warp speed, flying through space. I am just eyeballs moving at warp speed. White dots... stars are whizzing by me on all sides. I can't believe this is happening again. This is so awesome.

I finally arrive somewhere and come to an instant stop. Directly in front of me is a large white dot on a black background. 'Oh, the Sun', and it explodes with a big bang!

Scene change.

I am surrounded by blackness. I am floating in space. I am just eyeballs floating in the blackness of space. I'm not at all frightened. This is amazing.

I am as relaxed as if I were sitting in my favourite chair in my living room.

I can see ahead of me a large wall of shimmering black velvet. It is huge. I think it's the background of space, literally.   The black velvet undulates while tiny sparkles occur all over its surface. I see twinkling diamonds on shimmery velvet. This wall seems to be breathing.

I know it can see me. It knows I am here. We are facing each other. This is a face to face meeting of some sort. It's a stand-off between me and something massive and alive.

Suddenly, I am immersed in a world of stunning visual patterns. This is the world of DMT visuals that are familiar to those who have experienced DMT for themselves. It is beyond my ability to describe the visuals accurately. They truly are impossible to explain in any language.

These visuals play out as a long psychedelic experience for me.   I am essentially just eyeballs in space, watching indescribable patterns of light unfold before me. There are several fantastic DMT Trip simulations that can be found on the Internet. I highly suggest watching a couple to get an idea of what the visuals look like to a psychonaut.

As the complex visuals morph from one to another, information is pushed through me at an exceptionally fast rate. My mind can read what the image is showing me.

'The trip' shows me an image. I recognize the information that's presented to me. Once I understand what I'm seeing, 'the trip' tweaks the image to give me even more information.

This entire level is one long process of me interpreting DMT visuals. These DMT visuals will continue for the next 25 minutes of clock time. From my point of view as the one having the experience, these 25 minutes will feel like millions of years by the end of this level.

It doesn't take long for the visuals to begin teaching me. In fact, there is a curriculum here. There are specific topics that will be explored.

The first topic that 'the trip' teaches me about is Language, and what it is used for. It doesn't teach me other languages like German or Chinese or Russian. Specific languages don't matter here. What matters is how language is used and how it can be used.

I'm taught that language is everything. Language is how humans have progressed as a society. Without language, I literally would know nothing. Everything I know, I know because of language.

Humans only know what they have been taught, and everything they know has been learned through language.

'The trip' now begins pushing multiple streams of information through me via the DMT visuals, and what unfolds over the next few million years, is my very own, personal re-education.

This DMT education will unbelievably mirror the actual education that I really received between the years 1972 and 1986. It begins with grade one and a few subjects. I learn the basics in topics such as math, geometry, geography, science, and history.

This education continues up through the grades, continually become deeper and thicker with knowledge. This information challenges much of what I have been taught in my 49 years as a human being. I am being presented an alternate education.

The visuals continue and I move up further through this new curriculum of what I consider to be truth. As I get to higher grades of school, I start to explore physics and chemistry. I am shown the differences between Truth and what I've been told by humans.

Language is used to lie. Using language is comparable to casting a spell. Magicians use words to achieve their goals. Words are magic. Words are spelled.

Language is the only magic capable of turning worthless lead into valuable gold.

This elevating through the curriculum continues far beyond what I have ever been taught in school, or anywhere else. This education lasts for millions of years and consequently contains the most information of all the levels I have ever visited while micro dosing DMT.

To illustrate the type of information that is pushed through me by the amazing DMT visuals, here is a list. It's not a complete list, to be sure, but it is accurate. As the experience continues to unfold, these topics are eventually taught to me, in depth, by 'the trip', whether I want the information or not.

The DMT visuals do not stop. I am exposed to anthropology, biology, ecology, epidemiology, geo-biology, geology, herbology, immunology, neurology, pathology, physiology, psychology, sociology, technology, and zoology... to name just a few.

These are not simply brief glimpses or shallow excursions Into these topics. DMT ensures that no stone is left unturned in any topic. This experience from the psychonauts point of view, my point of view, lasts for millions and millions of years. Throughout this time, I am being shown images and patterns that feed me the information at computer-fast speeds.

My recently new, deep understanding of language is the important key to understanding all the information that is being pushed through me at lightning speed.

I can see all the examples that occurred during my life when language was used to lie to me about BIG things, important things. I understand how all my beliefs, everything I think I know as a human being, have all been shaped by the magical words of other humans.

The experience continues to dazzle my eyeballs and even more subjects appear in the stream of data that blasts through my open mind.

I begin to explore the Arts. Literature, prose, sculpture, dance, music, painting, photography, and others. I understand how the Arts play a role in carrying culture and history forward in time. Art is language that has been captured in a form that will outlive its creator. Art can last for thousands of years or more. Art is a very powerful form of language. The Arts keep society on a specific course. Art is beautiful to experience, but it also has a very specific purpose that lies deeply buried beneath the delicious surface.

I wonder how long I've been doing this. It seems like forever. Don't I have to work at some point?

My eyes fly open, and I am instantly smacked in the face with orgasmic bliss. My room looks completely normal. I can feel myself still at peak orgasm, ejaculating. I look down at my body to confirm this. I look at my clock.

Clock says 0210 hrs.

I've been at this for 70 minutes. This is unreal!

I also realize that even with my eyes open, I am still experiencing every bit of the education that up until now was only a 'closed eye' event.

I am acutely aware that my mind is somewhere else, perhaps hyperspace or Heaven or another dimension, while my human body sits propped up on my bed. With my eyes open, I see my room but feel the psychedelic experience that is occurring in my mind. I feel the visuals and soak up the data even though my eyes are open.

That part of me that I have always thought of as my mind or maybe even my brain... the thing that sits between my ears and behind my eyes... and does all my thinking... and contains all my memories... that thing is not currently located in my human body. This is my Soul. It is not currently located in my body.

When my body opens its eyes, it allows my Soul to remotely see out of my human eyeballs, in real time, from hyperspace... or wherever my Soul is at this moment. My Soul is still experiencing a massive re-education in the realm of hyperspace. However, when I open my eyes, my Soul sees my bedroom through my human eyes.

This understanding of the difference between having my eyes closed versus having them open is a mind blowing moment for me, the psychonaut.

I realize that I can mentally be somewhere in hyperspace, and still operate in the real world. I can function in my bedroom while my mind is off in hyperspace having an indescribable spiritual experience.

I can open my eyes and pick up my guitar and let my hands just go free and play, while mentally, I know that I am in some other dimension of reality.

I know that I can create beautiful music in this situation. I can just let creativity take over and allow the magic to happen.

This is without a doubt, one of the most fantastic situations a human being can find themselves in. You are literally connected to the Source and simultaneously allowed to use your human body.

Time is very interesting during this bridging of hyperspace with reality. With my eyes closed, it felt like millions of years were passing by. It seemed like it would never, ever end.

With eyes open, one may expect time to go by in a more normal fashion, perhaps more in step with the actual clock. Incredibly, this is not the case. With eyes open, the psychonaut experiences hyperspace time, not real time. I enjoyed thousands of years of playing guitar, in less than 2 minutes. I watched colourful ribbons of magic enter my fingertips from the air in my bedroom. I cried tears of joy and said thank you several times.

I continue to look around my room and wonder how I could ever explain this to anyone. There's not a single human that will ever believe this. I am literally on a bridge between hyperspace and normal reality.

The hyperspace education continues regardless of anything I do in my room. I find myself thinking about the occult. I realize that whatever I'm doing right now certainly counts as something occult. I am in 2 different places or dimensions at the same time.

I sit at a place where magic is possible. Real magic, not bullshit magic. This is where the occult lives. Occult topics are born here, where I sit. This is where magicians really exist. Sitting on the 'bridge' opens the door to real magic that has been hidden from us for a long time.

Language is where lies lay. I understand the depth to which I have been lied to.

To say anymore about this level would jeopardize the future existence of this very document.

I begin to feel the elevator slowing down. I no longer feel that I'm rising as I have been all along. I can feel the bliss fading away.

I recognize the trip is ending for me. I remember that I was smoking DMT. I can see it sitting on the table with my vaporizer. I listen to hear if anyone is in my apartment. It sounds quiet. I look at my clock.

Clock says 0215 hrs.

I seem to have as much time as I want, and the apartment sounds quiet. I can't come up with a good reason not to go even further. I'm all by myself and time is on my side, so why not keep going.

I scoop up another initiating dose of DMT, remove the whip from atop the bowl, and dump about 60mg in on top of the used, warm contents. Quickly I replace the whip. I know I only have a few seconds to get more DMT in me, or this won't work.

Immediately I inhale a big hit and start holding it for 10 seconds. I blow it out. I repeat this twice. I sit back and check the clock.

CHAPTER 8 - MY SKY

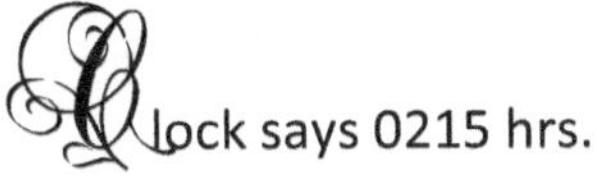lock says 0215 hrs.

I can now feel myself rising again. I can feel peak orgasm returning. The trip is starting all over again. I begin ejaculating again.

I can't believe it. This all started 75 minutes ago. I feel like it has been millions and millions of years that I've been doing this.

I have discovered something that will blow the world's mind... and I know that nobody will believe me. I understand why too. This is the craziest shit ever. I know.

Suddenly, I feel like a giant invisible hand has picked me up and loaded me into the chamber of a rifle. I forgot about this.

I'm launched.

Stars are flying by me. I am travelling at warp speed again. I remember this. I know this has already happened... some number of times. White dots... stars are whizzing by me on all sides. I can't believe this is happening again.

This time, I know what is coming. I know what sits at the end of this launch into hyperspace. It's not a sun or a white dot. I know this now, and I am ready for it.

I finally arrive somewhere and come to an instant stop. There it is. This is the actual, real, one and only Big Bang that is responsible for human consciousness. It explodes with a flash.

Scene change.

I am surrounded by the blackness of outer space. Eyeballs sitting comfortable on my chair, in outer fucking space. There are stars all around me in the distance.

I know that no one else on Earth is doing this right now. I'm the only human doing this. The sense of pride that I feel is out of this world. I know that I did something to cause this to happen. I'm the only reason that I'm sitting in outer fucking space right now. I did this myself without the help of any human. Nobody helped me get here. I did this all by myself. I just don't remember what I did to get here. I know it started in my bedroom.

As I sit relaxed in space, I see there's nothing happening. After about 15 minutes of floating, I hear a male voice inside my head. He encouragingly says, "Go explore!"

It hadn't occurred to me that I was free to just go. I immediately do what anyone would do, given the chance... I explore outer space.

The first thing I try to do is to go straight ahead, all the way to the far back wall of space. I immediately find myself there, at the back wall of space. I can touch it. It's a wall, hard to the touch, very smooth like glass, and cold.

I only needed to have this happen once, and now I am going everywhere, seeking the walls of outer space. It's all about finding the walls and touching them. I zigzag back and forth, all in the blink of an eye, and at the speed of thought. I do this for a long, long time... and I love it. This is the most fun I've ever had in my life!

There are celestial and cosmic bodies within this outer space that I'm exploring, but I care not for any of them. I completely ignore all the planets and moons and suns. I only have one desire and that is to figure out the true size of outer space. I want to know how wide and tall and deep it really is. I completely ignore the contents of outer space... I just want to know how big space is.

I place one hand on the right wall of space. I put another hand on the left side. I touch the back wall of space with my left foot. Finally, in a moment of humorous behaviour, I stick my tongue out and touch the wall in front of me. I'm touching all 4 sides of outer space at the same time.

I spend millions of years going back and forth trying to calculate how big outer space is. I consider several possible formulae that may explain how I am getting from one side of space to the other in seemingly no time at all.

I spend all my time attempting to measure space. I realize it is far smaller than I was told. It is also shallower than I expected.

I'm proud of myself for figuring things out. This level is truly playtime for me, and it seems to last as long as I want it to last.

I remember that I'm sitting on my bed and then I think about work later. My eyes spring open! I am smacked in the face with bliss beyond explanation. My room looks totally normal. I am at peak orgasm and ejaculating continuously.

I begin weeping joyously and thank an invisible someone. I say thank you, over and over again, alone in my room. Someone who loves me is allowing me to experience all of this. I'm the only person doing this right now. I love whoever is responsible for this. I thank 'Them'.

I enjoy this bliss for a while and then sadly, feel the trip coming to its inevitable end.

I begin to feel the elevator slowing down. I no longer feel that I'm rising as I have been all along. I can feel the bliss fading away.

I recognize the trip is ending. I listen to hear if anyone is in my apartment. It sounds quiet. I look at my clock.

Clock says 0240 hrs.

I have tons of time before I need to go to work, and the apartment sounds quiet. I can't come up with a good reason not to go further. I'm all by myself and time is on my side, so why not keep going.

I scoop up another initiating dose of DMT, remove the whip from atop the bowl, and dump about half of my remaining DMT in on top of the used, warm contents. Quickly I replace the whip. I need to be fast, or this won't work.

Immediately I inhale a big hit and start holding it for ten seconds. I blow it out. I repeat this twice. I sit back and check the clock.

86

CHAPTER 9 - MY UNIVERSE

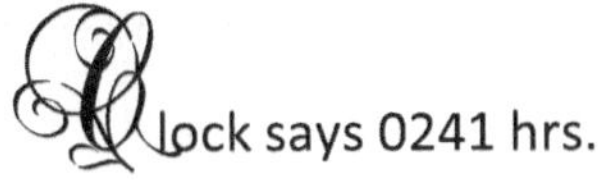 lock says 0241 hrs.

I can feel myself rising again. I can feel peak orgasm returning. The trip is firing up. Ejaculation resumes.

I can't believe it. I started this trip 100 minutes ago.

And then I feel a giant invisible hand pick me up and load me into the chamber of a rifle. It feels like my Soul is being rotated ninety degrees within my body. I remember this from before. I'm not a fan of the rotating soul feeling, but it lasts only two or three seconds.

I'm launched with a fury.

Stars are flying by me. I'm at warp speed again. I remember this. I know this has already happened... some number of times. White dots... stars are whizzing by me on all sides.

I know what's coming. No human would believe me, but I am about to witness The Big Bang, again.

I finally arrive in front of it and acknowledge it. It explodes with a tremendous flash.

Scene change.

I am surrounded by the blackness of outer space. Eyeballs sitting comfortably on my chair, just hanging out in space.

This place is very familiar although there is something different. I am no longer 'rising'. The sensation of going up has disappeared. I sense that I've hit some sort of ceiling.

There are stars all around me in the distance. Something new is here with me. To my left, in front, and below me, I see one large planet or moon. Something celestial and ball shaped. I can't give it a name. It's the size of my fist at an arm's length.

I just sit and enjoy the view. I wonder what's happening now. This feels like the same place that I just was. I'm pretty sure I've already been here. Yes, there is this new planet or moon, but it still feels like the exact same place I was just at. I'm not going up anymore.

I sit in space for a while. I wonder if I'm supposed to do something, or do I just sit here.

After some time, I begin to wonder where I am. I know I'm in space, but why am I here? How did I get here?

I decide to turn and look behind me. To my amazement, I can see a long yellow brick staircase extending down from where I am in space, all the way to a tiny man lying on a tiny bed… far below me. This staircase gently curves through the blackness of space, logically joining Me with me. I can clearly see how I arrived here. I came up the staircase one step at a time, and now here I am. It's not rocket science.

But as I look down at myself lying on my bed, I realize I can see the God Level also on this yellow brick staircase. It appears as a checkpoint, or a landing on the stairs, and is above the man on the bed. I recognize how the God Level is above the human level. I can see it visually represented on this staircase.

And now, even further up, and closer to me on this yellow brick tether of steps, I see a landing that represents My World. It's literally shown as a small image of Planet Earth sitting on the staircase, about halfway to me. As I consider this situation, I watch as the small Earth image begins to grow in size. It finally expands to envelop the God Level and the naked man on the bed, me. God and I are now contained inside Planet Earth. I am of course amazed by the sight of this.

The process continues with a new development on the staircase, located between Planet Earth and my location in space. At this high up landing on the steps, I see several twinkling stars. It looks like a starry night, but only on the stairs at this landing. A small dense cloud of stars marks the location of my Space Level. As I realize this, the cloud of stars begins to grow until it finally wraps around Planet Earth, which contains God and me.

This is deep. Nobody will believe it.

I remember God saying nobody would believe me. I also know that if I remember any of this when I wake up, I will tell people.

What if I forget all of this? That would be so sad to have no memory of any of this. That would be a horrible trick if I forget this.

I say to myself, "Please don't forget this, Buddy."

And then I sense that I need to turn around. I instantly spin myself in space and find that a woman has appeared from nowhere. She closely stands in front of me, looking up with brown eyes and a closed lip smile. She has long hair and is wearing a short black dress. She looks at me smiling and I look at her wondering who she is.

She says nothing, but I can tell that she is really happy to see me. She's beautiful and this is an incredibly picturesque location for this to be happening. I'm in no hurry for this moment to end, so we stare into each other's eyes for a while.

Suddenly, she grabs my right hand and says, "Come with me."

Scene change.

I am eyeballs sitting comfortably on my chair in the blackness of space. Directly in front of my eyes, a large viewing screen has been placed. I am watching a woman in a black dress and a naked man, while they chase each other through the blackness of space.

They play like children, trying to catch one another. They circle planets and moons and then dart off in another direction going deeper into the cosmos.

I can feel all the emotions that the naked man is experiencing. I'm sitting comfortably on my chair in space, watching television, and I can feel the experience just as if I were playing tag with this woman, in space. This is truly, the ultimate in virtual reality.

We are swimming through space. This isn't just empty space. We are moving in some form of liquid. We don't run or fly like Superman; we swim as if we are under water without the need to breathe. We move through this liquid with the speed and grace of dolphins.

Every time we touch, there are sparks, and we both experience a brief and intense orgasmic flash. Neither of us is really concerned about escaping the other. This is the fun.

She entices me further and further away from where we started this game. I follow her wherever she leads me.

Occasionally, she stops and turns to look at me. She waits for me to say or do something, and then we take off again when I say and do nothing.

Eventually, we both stop and look at each other. I realize this woman is not only my friend, but she is my best friend.

She has always been my friend. I understand that she waits here for me when I'm gone.

She smiles up at me. I can feel an upsurge in energy. Something is building. There is excitement in the air.

I have known this woman forever. When I am human, she is here all by herself, patiently awaiting my return. She has always been here for me.

I remember that I have returned to this woman thousands of times before this moment. She is always the woman who meets me.

I understand that this beautiful woman waits only for me. She serves no one else, just me.

As she looks up at me with excitement, her smile grows. She nods her head and asks me, "Have you figured it out yet? Do you know who you are?"

I have been trying to figure out who she was, but now I consider her question.

I think about everything that has happened today. I think about that yellow brick staircase. I remember God telling me that it's always been me. I remember millions of years of God's knowledge being pushed through me, undoing so much of what I had been taught by humans.

I finally fucking get it. I get it now. I am God.

My friend explodes with glee and quickly grabs my hand and drags me off deeper and further into the Universe.

She eventually encourages me to use my newly remembered powers. She reminds me that I can do anything. The Universe is mine to command she says.

I still don't believe it.

She says, "Start small and work your way up."

I think back to Level Three. I realize that I know everything, including how to create planets.

I simply think to myself, I want a Planet, and it magically appears in front of me. It blows my mind. I do it again several times.

I continue creating planets for a while. My friend keeps me company while I work my magic.

I again refer to Level Three and decide it's time to populate these lifeless spheres. At the speed of thought, I create life where there was none.

I create solar systems with multiple planets, all with life. Out of nothing I build galaxies filled with trillions of planets, all teeming with life.

I create anything I wish.

I spend billions of years doing this, and then I remember I have to work later today. I need to check the clock.

My eyes fly open. I am smacked with orgasmic bliss! My room looks normal. I don't hear any doctors or police in my apartment. I am still ejaculating.

I look to see how much DMT I still have sitting on the table. I see none. I thought I had some left.

I can feel the trip dissipating. The bliss fading. I don't have any more DMT so I can't do it again. I'm done. I wonder what time it is.

Clock says 0306 hrs.

Over the next 60 seconds, I become completely sober. In fact, I soon feel like a new man, fully refreshed and full of energy.

I jump up out of bed, grab a drink, and make a sandwich because I'm starving.

Eventually, I shower and go to work.

This concludes the trip report of my very first MdDMT experience.

What you've just read is my true story.

CHAPTER 10 - MY THOUGHTS

*W*ell, that is the end of 'the trip'. Let's talk about it.

I expect there will be some disagreement on what just happened to me. I know that some readers will have started reading this book with their own foreknowledge of what Kundalini is. I know others will not have had any prior exposure to the term Kundalini.

To those who have never heard of Kundalini before, I say welcome!

What you have read is an accurate description of Kundalini, written by a human (me) who experienced it personally. I've given what I consider to be one of the best contemporary descriptions of a Kundalini Awakening that you will find.   I've said it using language of the 21st Century, simple to understand and not buried beneath mumbo jumbo. I'm not attempting to conceal anything from you.

I want you to understand this experience as much as possible without having to do it yourself. To do so, I must be honest with you.

Let's face it, anybody can do this themselves. If I am lying to you... making all of this up... I will be found out. There are dedicated and courageous psychonauts out there that will find out whether I am telling the truth or feeding you all bullshit. In the end, if this book is bullshit, then it will not survive. I would be a fool to write anything but the truth if I want this book to live on beyond me.

Kundalini is quite literally an invisible, but real staircase that starts with each of us and leads up into the Heavens. It is always there for each of us to climb. I know we aren't taught that, so I'm saying it now. Of course, I know that sounds crazy. You would be quite normal if you think that sounds totally bat-shit crazy. For the first 49 years of my life, I would have scoffed at the idea of an invisible staircase right along with you. I believed what I had been taught.

And then one day, I climbed that staircase myself and that's how I know about Kundalini. I didn't compile the works of other's or do research to populate this book with interesting occult references. This is not a retelling of the same story you've perhaps heard before.

My only source for this entire book is the Kundalini experience itself.

I need to say that the Kundalini experience exists in every human being. Kundalini does not exist in the drug DMT. Many people assume that a DMT experience is within the drug itself. This is incorrect.

There is no more psychedelic experience existing within DMT than in a butter knife or automobile tire.

DMT's magic is its ability to activate specific receptors in the human brain. If the correct combination of receptors is achieved, this will activate the Kundalini experience that is in each of us. Micro dosing DMT achieves the correct combination of human receptor activation.

The standard, typical method of smoking DMT does not achieve the correct combination to open the door to Kundalini. While smoking DMT certainly lights up the human receptor network and results in fantastic, mind blowing adventures, it simply does not deliver the perfect, winning combination one needs to trigger the Kundalini experience.

Kundalini is a series of steps that go from a human's base chakra, all the way up to the top of the staircase. There is literally a top to a Kundalini experience. These steps do not simply go on forever. They do end.

Just as any other staircase has a first step at the bottom, and a last step at the top, Kundalini also has a first and last step. Also, just as with any staircase, if you only go partially up and then stop, you will not make it to the top.

Kundalini is like a 15 course meal, prepared by a world-famous Chef. The Chef prepares a specific multi-course meal that begins with hors d'oeuvres and ends with a flaming desert. The Chef expects the guests to eat their entire meal, start to finish. Nobody should be leaving part way through the meal. The Chef expects everyone to work through each course until they reach the end.

Kundalini wants the psychonaut to get all the way to the end as well. A partial Kundalini experience is not the goal of our Creator. Only once the psychonaut has taken that last step and finds they have arrived at the top, with nowhere else to go, will the Kundalini experience be brought to its final and inevitable conclusion.

The trip report that I presented earlier covered the first 5 levels or steps of my first MdDMT session.

My second MdDMT session took me even further up the staircase, perhaps twice as far as the first session.

Following two successful sessions, I was feeling on top of the world. I felt like I had discovered a magic portal that I could open anytime and then just go through to another incredible world where I could party with the best of 'em for millions of years... and still make it to work on time.

But after the second session there was a problem. In addition to everything wonderful that I remembered about the trips, I also remembered that the trips both ended horribly for me.   I couldn't remember exactly what happened to me on these two occasions, but I certainly knew without a doubt that each of those two sessions ended with me begging the experience to stop.

Would you be surprised if I did it again? Well, I decided to limit myself to just a first level experience for my third session. I hid my excess DMT in a tree stump a fair distance from my location. This ensured I wouldn't go beyond level one. This experience was wonderful.

A fourth session followed, and I chose to again stop at level one. I did not want to risk going any further up because I still knew that something bad occurred way up somewhere on the first two trips.

With four successful Kundalini sessions under my belt, I felt like a literal, real Magician. Not just a Magician, but the world's most powerful Magician. And I don't mean stage magic, I mean real magic.

Unfortunately, with this unlimited confidence and ego, I also became careless and didn't follow my own rules for micro dosing. I was so sure of myself that I eventually screwed up.

Kundalini was waiting for my error and jumped at the chance to teach me a lesson. My fifth session will be my last.

What was my mistake? Well, I started with 600mg of DMT. That was my first problem. And when it came time to load the vaporizer bowl, I was lazy. I didn't weigh the proper amounts out for myself.

 I made the mistake of dumping the entire 600mg of DMT into the vaporizer bowl. In my mind, I was sure that I could accomplish everything with one huge bowl of DMT. I felt that I was beyond needing to weigh the drug. I was expert at this. I had it all figured out and under control. I will throttle my usage.

Those who are familiar with DMT probably recognize that I was setting myself up for a disaster. A 600mg dose is ten times more than a standard break through dose. In the world of psychedelics, this is known as a 'stupid dose'. It was three times more than what was needed to successfully micro dose DMT. My life would be changing shortly.

My plan was to sip DMT from the whip for an hour and then take several big initiating hits to start the trip. That's what I did the previous four sessions. It is a very simple process. How could I screw it up?

Well, I don't remember anything from the micro dosing phase of session five. Once the experience was over, I would remember nothing about how I did it or what caused the malfunction.

It is only because I set up my phone to record the event that I have any knowledge of what I did wrong.

Let's look at the video evidence.

The micro dosing phase began as usual. I started inhaling small sips of DMT, holding them for a 10 count before exhaling. I continued repeating this for an hour. It was at this point that I should be inhaling the big initiating dose to begin the trip. Instead, the recording shows that I am just looking around my room while I sip and count. I continue the process for much longer than I should have. This becomes the problem.

Nobody ever told me what would happen if I 'went too long'. At the 125 minute mark of micro dosing (65 minutes too long), something happened.

After mumbling to myself for over two hours, my body eventually reaches what I call the 'critical saturation point'. I have too much DMT floating around in my system. I am literally overdosing on this drug. I am stepping over a line that I never saw coming.

At precisely 125 minutes in, my eyes closed for two seconds. Just two seconds, it was a slow blink. Then my eyes flew open, I jumped out of bed, grabbed my beautiful new vaporizer and all my DMT... and threw it all in the toilet. Something happened in that tiny two seconds of shut eye. I was happy for two hours, then BOOM... two seconds, done.

Please join me as I foolishly catapult myself into the longest two seconds of my life.

CHAPTER 11 - MY DEATH

I find myself sitting on a chair in my bedroom.

Directly in front of me is a naked me lying on the bed, smoking DMT from a vaporizer.

My bedroom doesn't feel right. It seems cold and sterile to me. It's very spooky to watch me on the bed doing drugs. I don't like it. In fact, I really don't like this situation.

This room has no love in it. There is nothing warm or friendly here. This feels like the worst place to be, and I really hate it.

I can feel a powerful energy in my room. It's not a nice energy. There is nothing nice about it at all.

I know that I did something wrong and that's why I'm here. I wasn't expecting this. I feel like I have made a horrible mistake and now I'm here.

The naked version of me, lying on the bed, is enjoying being god. That's what he's doing.   He's creating life throughout the Universe. What a wonderful god he is.

Simply by wishing it to be so, he creates planets and then populates them with life. He doesn't do much else with his newly inherited powers.

I watch from the safety of the chair in my bedroom as the naked man continues to marinate in his own godly bliss.

I am disgusted by myself. I'm watching an addict. What a piece of shit. How could I turn into that?

Time seems to stand still as I watch myself on the bed. The aura of this room is absolute evil. I can feel myself becoming more and more terrified and that is terrifying.

As the fear increases, I know it's not going to stop... and that makes it worse. Adrenaline or receptors or something is responsible for this steady increase of fear. Nothing scary is happening in my room, but I think it's the center of all things evil. There is nothing good in this room. Nothing. I hate it. I want this to stop.

Time doesn't seem to move ahead. I feel stuck in this. I'm being enveloped by an evil blanket, and it won't stop.

I'm a mouse surrounded by cats.

I try to convince myself that everything will be alright if I just sit and wait. Visually, I see no threats. My room appears to be safe. There really isn't anything to fear. I just need to wait for this to end.

But then the experience decides to shift gears. Apparently, I need to be shown what that god on my bed is doing.

What is he smiling and moaning about? That version of me is totally happy. He loves all this, and I do not. What is he so happy about? This place is devoid of anything nice, and it feels like a disgusting sewer to me. What is wrong with him?

Suddenly, I'm shown what's wrong with him. I'm forced to look at what that naked god in my bed is doing in the privacy of his own mind. What I see is repulsive to me. It makes me want to throw up. I am watching him create worlds full of life... for the sole purpose of harvesting their energy.

He makes a planet, covers it in life, and then simply commands that life to suffer. He funnels all that suffering into himself... he soaks in the suffering. He loves the energy that is beamed to him from each suffering planet that he created moments earlier.

He doesn't create humans or animals... nothing that complex. He simply 'creates life' on a 'planet' and then makes it suffer.

His goal is to get the energy. Earlier, he enjoyed harvesting energy from happy planets. He started out creating worlds with beautiful, happy life on them. He loved harvesting 'love energy' from his creations. He was a nice god at one time. But now he disgusts me absolutely. He creates suffering only to bath in it.

There are no words that I can use to explain how I felt when I realized the true situation here.

Of course, I recognize who that beast on the bed is. That disgusting sack of shit is me. There are really no words to express how disappointed I am to see my true behaviour. I, not someone else, am the worst god possible. I am nothing but pure evil.

I get so angry at myself I just want to get off this filthy chair and go over to the bed... and beat the shit out of me. But I can't get out of my chair. I'm just eyeballs. I can only watch the horror.

I am so ashamed of my behaviour... and I know that God knows what I have done. My behaviour is a deliberate, specific insult to my real God. I know that.

Yeah, I know that, but the naked fucker on the bed continues to love everything he's doing. That fucking smile on his face... the drool. I just want to kill him. He knows better. He's not stupid. He used to be a good boy.

I'm stuck here and I can't go anywhere else. I must watch me. It makes me sick.

I spend a long time watching me, and from my chair, I yell at me the entire time.

"You sack of shit mother fucker. You shouldn't be allowed to live. You absolute piece of dog shit. You fucker! You should be destroyed! You don't deserve to live. You should be removed from existence you fucking, dirt bag, piece of shit. God should just annihilate you from history you fucking bastard!"

I continue to berate and insult and threaten that beast on the bed for a long, long time. My verbal attacks become so vicious that I won't include them here. I become incredibly nasty as I attempt to slice and dice that son of a bitch with my words. There's no need to include that language here. Just know that I tried to destroy him with my words.

I know he is me. I'm not scared. I am seeing the real me. I hate him. I am full of hate towards myself. If I could physically be violent right now, I would tear that fucking prick apart with my hands... just so I could flush that shit down the toilet.

I beg God to eliminate me. Please destroy me. My soul must be destroyed forever... you can't let me continue. Remove me from everything. I should not be allowed to exist.

There is no soul worse than mine. Get rid of me now. Destroy that fucking animal. He should have never been allowed to live.

Scene change.

I am in outer space. I am playing tag with my girlfriend. She leads the way through the Cosmos and I follow. Our blissful game has taken us far into the depths of the Universe.

We eventually get to a place where there are several moons lined up in a row. In fact, there are two rows of moons in front of us. One row to the left, and one to the right.   My friend leads me between these two rows of moons.

As we move forward, I look to my left and see a moon. It has a face. It smiles at me. I then look to my right and see another smiling moon. My friend continues pulling me forward past several moons on both sides. Every moon has a face with eyes, a nose, and a mouth. Each moon is happy to see me.

I'm not sure how many moons there were. I would say 10 to 20 per side.

I don't recognize any of the moons, but they certainly know me. I can tell they respect and welcome me. This is a rather regal and exciting moment. These moons are all lined up here because they've been expecting me. This really feels like an important official event that I'm attending.

As we near the end of the smiling moon welcoming committee, my girlfriend turns around and we stop. She looks up at me and smiles.

She gives me a few moments to think about everything.

I turn around and look at the moons that I just passed. They are still looking at me and smiling. Why is this happening? I turn and look at my playmate.

She sweetly asks, "Have you figured out who you are?"

Its something she has asked before. In an attempt to formulate an answer for her, I begin thinking about everything that's happened so far.

It all comes together for me. I finally get it. I know who I am. I look at her and she's really, really excited.

I finally realize I am the one and only Lucifer. And guess what everybody... I fucking love it! Now I understand why I do what I do!

To celebrate my new identity, I start creating planets... with life.

Scene change.

I am sitting on a chair in my bedroom. I am more terrified than ever. I am fucking losing it.

That fucking animal is on the bed enjoying himself... knowing who he is. That bucket of garbage fucker. I want to kill him so badly. Let me destroy that piece of shit. Please God... let me destroy that beast. He shouldn't be allowed to live another second. He should be removed from all of history. He needs to be kept from the future. Please abolish that horrible soul once and for all.

May God have no mercy on your pathetic weak soul, you satanic piece of shit.

And then something changed. I watched that animal on the bed experience an epiphany. He stopped creating and thought about the situation.

In an instant, the animal realized what he has been doing all along. In this moment he truly understood the gravity of the situation.

I watch as that bastard begins begging God to stop all this. He's apologizing to God. Please, I'm sorry. I'm sorry. I'm sorry.

He begs for God's forgiveness for millions of years. He pleads to God to end this trip. Please, make it stop. Please, make it stop.

Now, from my point of view, sitting in the chair as just eyeballs... I see an animal, in pain, on my bed. The pain is so great that he is begging to die. He wants to be exterminated.

I remember the pain. The pain of learning that your true, God given identity is 'Lucifer'... is unbearable. Knowing that you've insulted God in the worst way possible is pain beyond suffering. I remember this because it happened to me. I am the beast in the bed. I am Lucifer, the one and only.

This was the horrible ending to my first two trips... that 'scary' ending that I could never remember. Those forgotten endings were my suffering at the realization of who I am.

I also remember his suffering will end once the drug wears off. I know he will be ok.

Unfortunately, he will do it again. When it's all over, he won't remember the eternity he spent begging for it to end. Without memory of that, he will do it again.

Scene change.

I'm sitting in a strange bedroom. It's not mine. From the decor, it's that of a teenage boy. His bed is made. He seems to be successful in something as there are trophies here and there. The room is very tidy. There is a desk and chair at the end of his bed.

I'm not sure why I'm here. Everything seems fine. This room Is warm wIth love and happy energy. I like it here.

Off to my right is the bedroom door. The door opens and a nicely dressed boy about fourteen years old walks in and closes the door behind him.

He tosses his duffle bag on the table and opens the zipper.

As I watch this boy, I simultaneously feel his emotions. He is excited with the thought of what he's doing, but he's also scared.

He reaches in the bag and pulls out a small container or jar. It fits easily in his hand, and he views it for a few moments.

I realize this boy is about to try drugs for the very first time.

Well, this will be interesting I think to myself. Let's watch this kid get high… see what happens. I don't know who he is. He's certainly not me. I have no trophies and I've never had a tidy bedroom. I don't feel any connection with this kid although I am stuck here watching him prepare his drug.

He knows his parents would kill him if they found out about this. He's scared of what the drug might do but he hopes everything will be alright. Friends have done it and they love it. He just wants to try it. He can always stop if he doesn't like it.

I continue to watch the show. This is very similar to watching a television program. I'm comfortable and safe where I sit. I'm not worried or scared of anything. Watching television is a very safe activity. He's the one doing the drugs, not me. I'm just going to watch. He can do whatever he wants. I don't care because it's not me.

The boy holds the drug in his right hand and pauses briefly while staring at the floor. Should he do it? Is this a bad thing? What if his parents find out about this? He knows he shouldn't do it, but he does anyway.

He moves his right hand to his left arm and touches the inside of his elbow with the drug. Well, that was easy.

Suddenly both he and I feel the incredible surge of bliss from the drug. He tosses his head back and smiles. I do the same.

What the fuck is happening? How is that possible? He did the drug and I felt it. I did not expect that.

I can't wait until he does it again.

Click.

I see the boy open the door and enter his bedroom. He goes to his table and retrieves his stash from his bag and hurriedly touches his arm with it. I love it. I feel it. I want him to do it again just so I can feel it again. I don't care about him. I just want to feel the rush of the drug. Come on buddy. Do it again.

Click.

I see the boy open the door and enter his bedroom. He goes to his table and retrieves his stash from his bag and hurriedly touches his arm with it. I love it. I feel it. I want him to do it again just so I can feel it again. I don't care about him. I just want to feel the rush of the drug. Come on buddy. Do it again.

Click.

I see the boy open the door and enter his bedroom. He goes to his table and retrieves his stash from his bag and hurriedly touches his arm with it. I love it. I feel it. I want him to do it again just so I can feel it. I don't care about him. I just want to feel the rush of the drug. Come on buddy. Do it again.

Click.

I see the boy open the door and enter his bedroom. He goes to his table and retrieves his stash from his bag and hurriedly touches his arm with it. I love it. I feel it. I want him to do it again just so I can feel it. I don't care about him. I just want to feel the rush of the drug. Come on buddy. Do it again.

Click.

I see the boy open the door and enter his bedroom. He goes to his table and retrieves his stash from his bag and hurriedly touches his arm with it. I love it. I feel it. I want him to do it again just so I can feel it. I don't care about him. I just want to feel the rush of the drug. Come on buddy. Do it again.

Click.

I realize that I have been repeating the same scene over and over and over. I feel like I'm stuck in a loop. This is horrible! I keep repeating the same 1 minute scene over and over.

And I love the feeling of the drug... but I hate the repetition. This looping is not a good thing. Something is wrong.

Click.

I see the door open and the boy walks in. He throws his drug on the table. He's excited and so am I. I know what's coming... and I love it. Come on buddy. Get that drug in us!

He taps his arm and we both get the rush. I fucking love this. This is incredible. I watch this kid get high and I get to feel it right along with him. This is pretty cool.

Click.

I see the door open and the boy walks in. He throws his drug on the table. He's excited and so am I. I know what's coming... and I love it. Come on buddy. Get that drug in us!

He taps his arm and we both get the rush. I fucking love this. This is incredible. I watch this kid get high and I get to feel it right along with him. This is pretty cool.

Click.

I see the door open and the boy walks in. He throws his drug on the table. He's excited and so am I. I know what's coming... and I love it. Come on buddy. Get that drug in us!

He taps his arm and we both get the rush. I fucking love this. This is incredible. I watch this kid get high and I get to feel it right along with him. This is pretty cool.

Click.

I see the door open and the boy walks in. He throws his drug on the table. He's excited and so am I. I know what's coming... and I love it. Come on buddy. Get that drug in us!

He taps his arm and we both get the rush. I fucking love this. This is incredible. I watch this kid get high and I get to feel it right along with him. This is pretty cool.

Click.

Am I looping? How many times have I done this? I feel like I've done this before. Something is wrong here. What's happening?

I've done this hundreds of times already. I know I have.
I've been doing this for a while.

Click.
The boy enters his messy room. He reaches in his pocket and pulls out our friend... the drug. He throws that into his arm and we both love it. I don't know who this kid is, and I don't care. It just feels so good!

Click.
Am I looping? How many times have I done this? I feel like I've done this before. Something is wrong here. What's happening?

I've done this hundreds of times already. I know I have.
I've been doing this for a while.

Click.
The boy enters his messy room. He reaches in his pocket and pulls out our friend... the drug. He throws that into his arm and we both love it. I don't know who this kid is, and I don't care. It just feels so good!

Click.
In a moment of clarity, I beg someone to make this stop. I can't take the endless looping. I have looped thousands of times. I am terrified and I want it to stop. I'm scared that it won't stop.

Click.
The boy walks in and I turn away. I don't want to see it. I want this to stop. He taps his arm with the drug, and I remember how wonderful it is. I love it!

Click.

In a moment of clarity, I beg someone to make this stop. I can't take the endless looping. I have looped thousands of times. I am terrified and I want it to stop. I'm scared that it won't stop.

Click.

The boy walks in and I turn away. I don't want to see it. I want this to stop. He taps his arm with the drug, and I remember how wonderful it is. I love it!

Click.

In a moment of clarity, I beg someone to make this stop. I can't take the endless looping. I have looped thousands of times. I am terrified and I want it to stop. I'm scared that it won't stop.

Click.

The boy walks in and I turn away. I don't want to see it. I want this to stop. He taps his arm with the drug, and I remember how wonderful it is. I love it!

Click.

I'm screaming please stop. Please stop. I get it! I get it! Please make this stop. I get it.

A stern male voice in my head bellows at me, "NO, you DON'T get it!"

Click.

I'm sitting in that boy's room again. The room looks like shit. He looks like shit. He's a fucking druggie now. He doesn't want to be a druggie, but he does love the drug. He slams another load into his arm and we both love it.

Click.
I'm sitting in that boy's room again. The room looks like shit. He looks like shit. He's a fucking druggie now. He doesn't want to be a druggie, but he does love the drug. He slams another load into his arm and we both love it.

Click.
I'm sitting in that boy's room again. The room looks like shit. He looks like shit. He's a fucking druggie now. He doesn't want to be a druggie, but he does love the drug. He slams another load into his arm and we both love it.

Click.
I'm sitting in that boy's room again. The room looks like shit. He looks like shit. He's a fucking druggie now. He doesn't want to be a druggie, but he does love the drug. He slams another load into his arm and we both love it.

Click.
Oh no I've been looping again. What is that... a few thousand times? Why is this happening? Did I break something?

No. Wait. Seriously, how many times have I done this? What the hell is going on? Doesn't this end? I don't want to be part of this anymore.

I start begging for it to end.

"Please make it stop. Please, I get it... I get it."

A stern male voice in my head bellows at me, "NO, you DON'T get it!"

Click.

I see the boy standing on the sidewalk in front of a public school. A young pretty girl walks up to him. She's nervous and excited. She hands our boy some money, and he gives her some drugs.

I realize that I'm in trouble. I have a feeling I know where this is going.

I start begging for it to end.

"Please make it stop. Please, I get it... I get it. I don't want to see any more."

A stern male voice in my head yells at me, "NO, you DON'T get it!"

Click.

I'm sitting in a strange bedroom. It's not mine. From the decor, it's that of a teenage girl. Her bed is made. She seems to be successful in something as there are trophies here and there. The room is very tidy. There is a desk and chair at the end of her bed.

The bedroom door opens and a nicely dressed girl about fourteen years old walks in and closes the door behind her.

She tosses her book bag on the table and opens the flap.

She reaches in the bag and pulls out the drugs that she purchased from our boy.

I realize this innocent soul is about to try drugs for the very first time in her life.

I scream at her, "Don't do it baby. Don't do it."

She touches the drug to her arm and we both love it. Yes. Do it again. I love it.

What followed was a repeat of what I went through with the boy and his drugs. Seemingly endless looping of the same event occurs over and over and over.

I realize that I've been doing this for a long time. I surface from the experience long enough to scream, "Please, stop. I get it! I get it!"

That voice in my head yells at me, "No, you DON'T get it!"

I return to the world of looping.

I realize that I've been doing this for a long time. I surface from the experience long enough to scream, "Please, stop. I get it! I get it!"

That voice in my head yells at me, "No, you DON'T get it!"

The loops continue. One small step by one small step, I watch this girl destroy her life.

I realize that I've been doing this for a long time. I surface from the experience long enough to scream, "Please, stop. I get it! I get it!"

That voice in my head yells at me, "No, you DON'T get it!"

Click.

I am in another bedroom. In bed are the parents of the girl. Her father is asleep, but mom is awake. She can't sleep. Her eyes are wide open in the darkness. She wonders what she did wrong. She loves her daughter more than anything in the world. She doesn't want her baby to die. She is tortured by her daughter's drug use.

I don't like what I'm seeing. This is painful... I don't want to see it.

The looping continues and I'm forced to watch mom thousands of times.

I realize that I've been doing this for a long time. I surface from the experience long enough to scream, "Please, stop. I get it! I get it!"

That voice in my head yells at me, "No, you DON'T get it!"

Click.
I'm at a funeral. Oh no. I begin crying. I see the mom and dad of the girl standing there. It is her funeral. This is a devastating scene to witness. I hate this.

Click.
I'm at a funeral. Oh no. I begin crying. I see the mom and dad of the girl standing there. It is her funeral. This is a devastating scene to witness. I hate this.

Click.
I'm at a funeral. Oh no. I begin crying. I see the mom and

dad of the girl standing there. It is her funeral. This is a devastating scene to witness. I hate this.

Click.
I'm at a funeral. Oh no. I begin crying. I see the mom and dad of the girl standing there. It is her funeral. This is a devastating scene to witness. I hate this.

After thousands of loops, I realize that I've been doing this forever. In complete terror, I scream, "Please, stop. I get it. I get it. I fucking get it!"

That voice in my head yells at me, "No, you don't FUCKING get it!"

Click.
I see the boy standing on the sidewalk in front of a public school. A young boy walks up to him. He's nervous and excited. He hands our boy some money and in return he gets drugs.

As I am about to start begging for this to stop, I realize that I finally do get it. I was lying every time I said that before. I just wanted the experience to end. I didn't care about the boy, or the girl, or the parents. I hated the looping and being forced to watch it. I would have said anything to get it to stop.

But now, I get it. I actually do understand.

For the first time in millions of loops, I don't beg for it to end. I simply say, "OK. I get it."

Scene change.

I am eyeballs in outer space. I'm flying straight ahead at a fast rate towards an object. It resembles a thin sheet of paper. It's wide and long, but there isn't much height.

I am rapidly approaching the thin edge of this sheet of paper. I quickly become concerned with my own safety as I am on a collision course with this skinny little edge.

As I approach the edge, I see no openings, no doors. I'm scared that I'm going to smash into it. I'm flying very fast.

Scene change.

I'm sitting on the floor of a green walled room in an old hospital. There is paint chipping off the walls. My room has windows that look out to a hallway. There is a fluorescent light above my head, flickering.

I see no signs of life in my area, but I do hear occasional noises from elsewhere in the hospital. I'm sure I'm not alone, but I see nobody else.

I feel like I really fucked myself up. I did something, and now I'm here. I did a drug... and it ruined my brain.

I did a drug and now I'm right here in some kind of a hospital nut house.

How is this possible? I used to work at a group home where I took care of people with mental problems. And now I'm one of them? I will never be normal again.

Why did no one ever warn me? I didn't know this could happen. What's going on in my head is so fucked up… there's no way I can live a normal life like this. I'm stuck in some psychedelic swirl of colors and thoughts… I can't think straight. My brain is bent in half. This is horrible. I feel like I've been here for hours.

They put me here, so I won't hurt myself. Will I ever be normal again?

No. I won't be normal again. This is it forever you stupid shit. You did this to yourself you fucking idiot. You fucked up… and now this is the result.

You did it to yourself. You're never going to eat or speak or walk or nothing. You fucked you up… nobody else did.

You loved your drugs didn't you buddy. Yep, you loved 'em.

Well, here you go buddy boy.

Enjoy your stay. You did it to yourself.

Scene change.

I'm standing on a path, in a clearing, in a forest. It is nighttime. My immediate vicinity is illuminated enough that I can see the path leading off into the woods ahead of me.

To my right side, there is a being standing by the right edge of the path. He appears to be half beast, half man, or he's just really hairy. He has some sort of armour on and he's simply standing at the side of the path with his arms folded across his chest.

He's looking directly at me with no emotions. He blinks and breathes as we both stare at one another. I don't know who this is.

Eventually I turn my eyes to the path. It's a dirt path that leads from me to the forest a short distance ahead of me. I can see that it goes into the trees and then quickly fades to black. Only the clearing where I stand is illuminated, and it's still only moon light bright. I have no idea where this path goes, but I'm standing on it.

I turn and look at the guard. He's still staring at me. He doesn't look angry. He looks bored.

I wonder what I'm supposed to do. Do I just stand here and wait? That guy isn't talking to me and nothing else is happening.

I'm glad nothing else is happening right now. I'm concerned that when something finally does happen, it won't be fun.

You know what. I think I'm just going to stand here on the path. I'll play the game. If nobody else is going to make something happen, then I'll just wait. I can wait for a long time. I'll let that guard stare at me forever. I don't care.

After about twelve hours of daydreaming while standing there silently on the path, I am exhausted. I turn and look at the guard. He's not looking at me. His eyes are aimed across the path and not at me. OK. Nice. Everything is stable. Nothing is happening. I decide to waste more of his time.   In fact, I stand there and think distracting thoughts for at least another 24 hours.

Nothing happens and nothing changes. Occasionally I look over at the guard who is completely uninterested in me.

But eventually, I start thinking more deeply about where I am and what is happening. I've been standing here for a long time. I'm getting tired of postponing the inevitable.

The truth is this. I figured out where I am within a few minutes of arriving here. As soon as I saw the guard on the path, in a clearing, in a forest, I knew where I was. This is why I don't want this process to go any further.

My plan is to drag this out as long as I can. So, I keep staring at the path in front of me. My mind is racing. I'm thinking about everything.

I know I've done this before and that makes me lose hope. This is not my first time here.   I've stood on this path, beside that guard, many times before. I am not going to win this battle. I never do. It always turns out the same.

I'm just not ready to do it yet. I continue to silently stand on the path for many more hours.

Out of nowhere, a bright golden rope appears in front of me. It is hanging in the air above the path. The rope begins near me, then coils into a large pile, and finally trails off and fades in the distance.

This rope is self illuminating and shines with an internal golden light. All along the rope are black lines that appear to separate the rope into segments. Every few inches there is a black line followed by a golden segment of some length. There are millions of segments on this golden rope and each one is separated by a thin black line.

As soon as I see this golden rope in front of me, I know what it is. I hate that this is happening to me, but I know what that rope is. I've seen it so many times before.

I don't want to admit that I'm here again. When I look at the golden rope suspended in front of me, I can see how many times I have been here before. Every black line on that rope represents a time that I stood right here on this path. Every golden segment represents a life I've lived.

Every life I've lived has been separated by this experience I'm having right now. I live a life, and then I'm here. Then I live again.

Look how many times I've been here. Every time I'm here, I do the same thing. I should be ashamed of myself for just standing here saying nothing.

I can't do this forever. I know I've always stalled and tried to waste time here, but I just don't have the strength to keep delaying this any longer.

I am about to start my fourth day of standing quietly on the path. I am tired of this.

I finally begin to do what I always do at this point. I start apologizing. I scan through my life and find things that I did wrong, and I apologize for them.

I begin with what I would call milder apologies and work my way up to larger, thicker apologies as I go.

Now, as the author, part of me wants to give you a list of my apologies. That would help set the tone for this section. But the truth is my apologies are mine. They would mean nothing to you. Imagine your own apology list if you must.

Each time I mention an event and say I'm sorry, a little piece of me is chipped away. Each apology breaks me down a little bit more.

Following hours of apologies, I am deep in it. I'm crying so hard I'm choking on my own saliva. My list of apologies is getting shorter... but I'm not done yet.

As more chunks of me fall away I feel like I'm breaking down. I'm breaking apart. Every apology breaks me up a little more. If I were a statue, imagine pieces of me falling away and landing at my feet.

After 24 hours of apologizing, I'm almost done. I'm running out of excuses. I'm tired of this. I'm exhausted.

I have been judging myself all along. I listened to each of my apologies, and now I judge myself.

Here's the thing. There's one apology that I always leave for the end. It's what I'm most ashamed of. It's my worst sin. Some may feel it is my only sin.

I'll waste as much time as I can with minor apologies as long as it delays this moment.

But in the end, I finally clear my throat and prepare to speak. I've said it millions of times before. This time will be no different.

I say, "I'm sorry Mommy. I did it again. I turned my back on you, and I'm sorry. Please let me try again."

I collapse from exhaustion.

Click.

I see a pile of bricks sitting on the path in front of me. These are black bricks with small areas of yellow showing through here and there. These are my bricks. That was me. That used to be my structure, my building, me. I destroyed myself.

This saddens me beyond description.

I look at my pile of dirty bricks. I remember when my bricks were yellow and clean. Now they're black and shitty.

Suddenly, a gigantic hand reaches down from the left side and scoops up my pile of bricks. This is God's hand. In one smooth move She slides her fingers under the bricks and without effort, lifts them up off the path.

She moves Her hand closer to my face so that I can see it better. She holds it there. I can see the black soot on my bricks.

I see Her chin appear as She leans Her head down to where I am. I see Her mouth and nose. This is our Mother, our Creator, our God.

From the left, She exhales a golden coloured cloud of diamonds and blows it at my pile of bricks. Her breath blasts all the black dirt from my bricks and the filth flies off to my right side.

I can feel a fuzzy buzzy sensation throughout my entire body.

She continues exhaling this golden breath and moves Her face, so She is opposite me, on the other side of my new pile of yellow bricks. Her breath passes over my bricks and hits me in the face.

This is the most spectacular moment in my life, ever. As my Mother's breath hits my face, I understand that She still loves me.

I fall backwards and hear my Mommy say, "You are reborn."

Scene change.

I'm at my living room ceiling, looking down on me lying on my couch.

I begin speaking from my position at the ceiling, "Yeah… I'm wetting myself… I understand. I got ya. Listen it's not funny. I got ya. I got ya. I'm shitting myself. It's not… I'm dying."

As I look down at me on the couch, I can sense that my Mom is right behind be. I haven't seen her for so many years and now she is right behind me.

I say, "Mom, I'm dying. Isn't that crazy. I did a drug… and now I'm dying. That's hilarious Mom. I fucked up and now I'm dying."

Click.
I am sitting with my parents in their home. My Dad sits across from me on his favourite chair. My Mom is to my right and further away. She appears to be preparing food in the kitchen. I sit on a couch.

I say, "I can't believe I died Mom. I took a drug and I died. That's so crazy. Just like that… I didn't see it coming."

"It's so nice to be here with you guys. I missed you. I did. I love you. I do. I killed myself though, didn't I?"

"I love you guys so much. I can't believe I'm here. I died and now I'm here with you guys."

This isn't any home that I recognize. I've never been here before, but it is wonderful, being with my parents again, regardless of where we are.

I stay here and talk for several hours until I finally curl up on their couch for a nap. I feel like I am home.

Scene change.

I'm surrounded by blackness.

An oval shape moves into my view and stops about twenty feet ahead of me. The oval has fuzzy edges and many sparkling diamonds within it. I don't recognize it.

The oval changes its look to that of my Mom. Now I see my Mom standing there.

I say to her, "What's going on Mom?"
She says, "You've got to go soon."

I consider what she says and realize that something does feel odd. I feel an electric fuzzy buzzy sensation building up around me.

"I don't have much time Mom."
"I know."
"I love you. It's nice being with you again. I don't want to go."
"Is there anything you want to ask before you go?"

I seem to have only one question that I need answered. I ask my Mom, "Can you tell me if Jesus is real?"

She smiles and steps to her left side. From behind her emerges an oval shape, a little shorter than my Mom.

This oval positions itself beside her, to her right side. The oval then appears to me as Jesus.

I see Jesus standing beside my Mom. My immediate reaction is to say, "Jesus Chri…"

I stop in mid exclamation and bow my head in shame.

I hear Jesus start laughing and my Mom joins in with Him. I realize I made a joke, and everyone is happy. The three of us laugh together for a few seconds.

But then I feel the fuzzy buzzy feeling getting super intense.

I feel myself rapidly moving backward and away from Jesus and my Mom. I hear her yell to me from some distance "You are going to get yourself a Bible."

Scene change.

I'm surrounded by complete blackness.

In front of me and up to my right, I can see a small man sitting on a small chair. His back is to me. He appears to be floating in this blackness, about 500 feet from me.

I recognize that man on the chair as me. I remember that I did a drug. I remember that some people get death trips. I can tell that I'm not *really* dead. I'm coming back to my body. I didn't really die!

I am so excited to actually not be dead.

It takes about sixty seconds for me to finally get up close to the man on the chair. This is a long and enjoyable out of body experience. I've always wanted to do this.

My eyes pop open. I pull the whip of my vaporizer out of my mouth and drop it to my side.

I snap up to a sitting position and begin speaking.

We're done. Jesus Christ, Bunn (my nickname)! You did. What the fuck happened. You gotta stop. Holy fuck. You just gotta come back to reality, Jesus Christ.

I stand up beside my bed. My cell phone video camera continues to record me talking to myself.

OK, so you'll be ok. Of course, you'll be ok.

Come back to reality.

People have been here a million times, but you gotta stop. You gotta come back... just. You're done... that.

It's only been... sometime... and you're done.

This is your apartment.

This is your apartment.

How dare you do that?

Now you come back to reality... and you get rid of that shit. You get rid of that shit.

Don't you ever do that again.

Just make sure everything's ok.

Now you gotta get your shit back together... and you flush that shit down the drain.

Don't you ever do that shit again. Don't you ever... do it again.

Never do it again. Never do it again.

That's it. Fix your fucking life.

I grab my camera and bark into the unforgiving lens, "Watch this once and fix your fucking life."

I open my bedroom door and step out for the first time in two hours. One of my cats is by my feet trying to trip me, the other two are nowhere to be seen.

As I walk to my living room, I drag one hand on the wall for support. I keep my eyes wide open and blink rarely. I don't want to close them any more than I need to. If I blink for too long, I might see something I don't want to see. I'm not sober yet.

I place my phone on the arm of my couch and leave it there recording.

I begin speaking to myself again.

It's all about time, now stop it.

You can never come back from here I mean you can never do this again never ever don't ever do this drug again.

I'll get rid of this.

I immediately stomp off to my bedroom and violently grab my wonderful new glass vaporizer, and my DMT... and I throw it all in the toilet.

Stop repeating. Listen Bunn, you don't like that fucking thing never do it again.

It's crazy.

Don't ever do it again, you're stuck in that fucking millions of years, Jesus Christ.

I return from my bathroom and pick up my phone. I find the Stop button and I press it.

This ends the video recording. It has been 6 minutes since my eyes opened from my two second death trip.

I sit on my couch and keep my eyes open. My cats join me. They seem to have had an experience themselves while I was gone. We are all happy to see each other.

I relax and consider everything that's happened. I have a lot to think about.

I experienced the exact thing I was hoping to avoid from the beginning. I had the death trip. Somehow, I fucked up and here I am.

20 minutes later and I am quite proud of myself. I know I did something that very few people ever do… and I know I don't have to do it again.

I'll never do it again. I already did it. I just did the unbelievable… and it happened. I was there. I did it and I survived.

I know I'll never do it again, and I'm happy with myself for that.

Now that it's over, I never have to do it again.

After about 30 minutes of thinking on the couch, I got up and turned on some music. I also clicked the television on and muted it. I wanted to hear familiar sounds and see some motion in my room.

I needed some activity to break the silence in my apartment.

My three cats keep me company as I sit and remember everything from my trip. I'm completely sober and the effects from the drug have all vanished.

I am so happy that I did the unthinkable, and now I'm done. It was terrifying but wonderful. I am definitely proud of myself.

And then suddenly, my vision and hearing became superhero level awesome. I could see the texture of the paint on the far wall of my apartment. I could hear the activity of everyone in my building. I heard pins drop. This increase in acuity occurred in an instant.

I could also feel a fuzzy buzzy sensation in the room.

I panicked. Oh no. It's not over. I already threw my shit out. I didn't smoke any more, did I?

This can't be happening to me.

The fuzzy buzzy sensation is intensifying. I realize that it's outside, not in my apartment.

I can feel that there is a circle of fuzzy buzzy energy that is surrounding my apartment. Imagine a huge doughnut of energy that is slowly shrinking around me. I can feel it coming closer from all sides. I am sitting in the center of this doughnut. I'm in the doughnut hole.

It doesn't feel close to me. It feels like this circle of energy is a mile wide and shrinking around me.

I was panicking but now I've taken an interest in this fuzzy buzzy energy. It feels so comforting and nice. It both grows in intensity, and shrinks in size around me, at a constant rate.

Wait a minute. I recognize this. How do I know this feeling? I've felt it before. How have I felt this before?

I start thinking about my life, trying to figure out when I've experienced this.

I think about the last few years. When I had my wisdom teeth removed? Nope.

I go further back. Was it that time I took mushrooms? Nope. What about that time I tried LSD? Nope.

Well now I'm thinking into my childhood. Was it that surgery I had? Nope.

The fuzzy buzzy seems to be getting a lot closer to my apartment. I can really feel it intensifying, but I'm not scared because I know it's happened before.

And then I remember. It makes me so happy to remember.

The last time I felt this fuzzy buzzy feeling was when I was born in 1967 at Grace Hospital, Windsor Ontario.

Now there are mixed emotions in me. I'm thrilled but terrified. Whatever is outside and getting closer... is almost here. This is really happening!

I know that something is about to happen, so I grab my phone and press the Record button.

I sit on my couch and stare at the screen door to my balcony. That's where it will happen. Whatever is out there will be coming through my balcony door momentarily.

The energy tightens around me.

And then in front of me there is a shimmering, sparkly oval shape. It flashes the human image of my sweet Mother

Jane for a couple seconds, and then changes back to an oval of energy standing in my living room.

Mom?

This is perfectly wonderful. I lie down on my couch and get comfortable. I hold my phone in my hands and continue recording. Wouldn't you?

What follows is a portion of the transcript of the conversation that I had in my apartment with my mom. She died 11 years ago, but has come to visit me today.

CHAPTER 12 - MY PARENTS

egin transcript:

Once the drug is over okay okay I got that.

Oh. Listen. This is your Mom for fuck sakes.

Okay I got you, I got you. I got you Mom.

Mom I'm recording... listen please Mom, Mom! I know you're there, Mom... or God wouldn't be able to put it to tape. You know Mom I gotta put it to tape Mom, I gotta catch this. I gotta catch me using this drug. I should have never used it listen like... I gotta catch this on tape though, and I hope you are.

Listen. This is going to tape, isn't it?

Yeah... I'm wetting myself... I got you, I got you! This isn't funny but as long as you're catching it... this is really...

All right.

I understand that it'll be over...

Just checking to make sure you're recording Mom.

I'm gonna get back to that Mom. I am so sorry. Listen, I have to make sure I'm recording because I am shitting myself... I'm dying!

Isn't that something. Okay. I get it, I get it. I have to give up what I just did... and I died. I fucked around... I get it. I fucked around and I'm coming home.

Okay.

I get it though. I get it Mom... as long as you're recording. Please make this be recording like I understand...

I do but just that fucking... how can... I just can't see!

It's all like... please fix that.

Can you just make it so that I can see? I know you're showing me something but show me...

Please show me Mom. I know I'm gonna watch this later, but I gotta get to this point.

Yeah.

I love you, Mom. I love you. I miss you I do.

I missed you, Mom.

Isn't that funny! That's fucking hilarious that... that uh... you know... I died Baby.

I miss uh... please, promise me that you're recording this. It wouldn't be happening, right, if... I get it but I died though, didn't I? And people say that because I was an idiot for doing this... this is what I gotta do.

This is it, and either I come to, or I don't, mm-hmm okay.

I love you, Mom. I love you, hmm thank you!

Please be recording... yes, is that... is that a square that means I can stop it? Right! Pause... does that mean its recording? Come on, because I just can't see it, that's all. You know... please... I love you Mom and I've learned some stuff, Jesus Christ!

Holy shit Baby.

Mama?

Oh my God, Baby. Are you still recording? Show me that. I just can't fucking see it. This is gonna blow my mind.

Yeah, and they say when you're done, you won't be able to remember... oh thank you.

Thank you, Mama. Oh, you're so beautiful. That's unbelievable Baby Baby Baby.

Mama!

Come on Bunn. Isn't that amazing! I had to give up all my egos like... who I am, because I love my Mama.

Mama... you are amazing Mama.

Oh, my God, are you still recording? Please let me check that. I can't even imagine... really?

Show me! Jesus... oh fuck... we always come back to the same shit, and as long as you're recording, please allow me to be straight enough to go to work later please.

Please, Mama.

Look at your picture up there on my wall. Why have I got all your pictures hidden in my closet?

Something...

... but you better fucking learn from this shit... and don't you be fucking... don't...

Okay make the deal, go, go... make the fuckin' deal yep. I'm...

New tape. This is for Buddy. This is for Buddy. Go, are we recording? Pause... is that what it says? Is that what it says? I just can't fucking see it!

Show me. Show me. Show me the goddamn thing. These are the eyes that you fucking made.

It better be recording. Does that say pause in a square... because that means stop and I can fucking, once and for all, stop worrying about it... and I know it doesn't really fucking matter if it's plugged in, or runs out of battery, because you, sweet Baby, are gonna make sure that it records because this is in Heaven, Baby, and you got shit to tell me, right, and...

I just want to make sure you get it on clock. Okay.

Where are we? Where are we? Where the fuck are we? Because Bunn... you know you're throwing this shit out. I hope you're showing this to Buddy, right?

Listen you... you fucking listen... you've already... I...

Okay. How many fucking times...

You got it. But you know what? I'm gonna spend... I'm gonna spend the rest of my fucking life telling you...

You better not do that drug again. You better not do that drug again. You better not do that drug again. You don't you dare, don't you dare.

Get this out while you're still fucking fried, because you're here for a million fucking years. A million years, oh yeah, catch it on tape fucker, because I'm sitting here with God, and I know...

Nope. Nope. All right.

This is... as long as I'm done. I already threw my shit in the garbage. You got that? You better be recording. Please, Buddy, you have to watch this sweet buddy... sweet buddy, listen...

Is that pause? Good, I got it for fucking once. Okay there we go. I can see the time... shit... are we just good, and...

We're good, yeah, I think we're good. Times... take a good...

Buddy, I can tell you this. I got forever, because I'm in that place. Don't you ever, don't you ever, do that drug. In fact... I'm full... I'm dead.

It's gone. I am never doing it again, and you know what?

You see this? That pause, and a square... that paused, and the square, and the time, and for fuck sakes, Bunn when you're... when you're sober, and you think, "hmm, maybe I'll watch this again." This ain't about other people.

Are you catching this Bunn? Because I know it's gonna end for me sometime. I just keep checking the clock.

I got ya! Just as long as you're catching this, on tape, please, and Mom... I'm back to you sweet Baby.

You know, I missed you. I just want to be with you, for a while, please Mama. I'm not gonna waste my time. Okay.

Buddy, listen, okay. Are you serious? You gotta learn from this, because it's over me, and I gotta learn from this. But I gotta make sure I give this to you sweet buddy. You gotta watch it, okay. You gotta watch it. You gotta fucking watch it. I'll be fucking...

I'm gonna start the tape again, just to make sure... okay. It is recording. Let's see the numbers going by.

It better be real, buddy, come on. Please be real. It won't even be on, I'll bet you that.

Come on, I know that though... the most important thing... Okay, fine. If you don't get rid of this shit, and never do it again...

You gotta be watching... gotta be watching... as long as this... as long as you're really doing it.

What if you're not? Jesus!

Okay, you got to make sure that you've... you got to make sure that you've uh... yeah, come on bud, write yourself a note. You gotta never do it again. You're gonna never do this again, Baby. You gotta never do this again... this is crazy... you never do it again.

Buddy, are you there?

There you go. You gotta be... you can't ever do this again buddy. That's why you smashed your stuff in the toilet. You became one, you fucking literally became one with... like a flat plane universe that never ever ends. You do not want to ever come back here, buddy.

You will throw your fucking life away, in one fucking day.

Now, I am your Mother. Thank you, mother speak through me, now mother. Speak through me, now. Fix my life Mama, please. I gotta make sure you're recording, because you know I love people. You know I love people. I love people.

Please, I gotta snap back to reality and check that the phone is recording. I want to check and see what kind of charge we've got going on, because I've been walking around with you for a long time. Okay but you appear...

Okay, I'm pretty sure we're good to go. Anyway, I love you Mom, and as the trip is over... I'm coming back to reality, but I want to close my eyes. I'm gonna spend the time with you.

Look at you, Mama. Please be recording. You're gonna watch this later Bunn, and you're gonna understand why you threw your fucking new vape in the goddamn toilet. And you're gonna have to figure out why you fucking did that, but...

Mama. Mama.

Okay, listen, you still got time Bunn. You still got time. This is your Mama talking to you, look. Come on, give me this. Look Baby. Look Baby, you...

Come on do it again. I know I can see it when I... I can see you in my phone, Mommy. Tell me, and I wish, I wish it would be you on my phone later, when you're giving me shit for doing this. This is gonna stop. Nowhere, never again baby Bunn. You're not Bunn, you're Aaron Bensette. Don't do it. Don't do it, again.

Mama? Hmm. You gotta watch this, Bunn. Okay, you are watching this, and Buddy... anybody... if you're gonna show anybody, Bunn... show people. It's not about you. It isn't, Baby.

Look at your Mama... look at... I am your Mama, right now. Your Mom is talking to you. Hmm, yeah, show people. Show people. This is reality. Gotta make sure the door is closed, I think it is.

It's your Mama, and then you're recording... please be recording... I gotta push it...

You know how important it is for me... listen. You know how important it is for me... look, I get it okay. I get it. You know if you don't watch this. I got you.

Please, I'm coming back, and I'm recording, I'm stupid... I'm just looking for...

I gotta explain what I'm doing, because I need your help, right now, I need your help, okay? Please? You see what I've done. You see what I've done, and I'm recording, and I have a little trouble right now finding the plug, to plug in, because I don't want you to ever leave.

I don't want you to ever leave Mama. I'm sorry about anything. That's stupid. I mean, I'm sorry for what I've done with my life... this!

I got you... I got. I gotta get those other shits, just fucking give them up. I got you, Mama. You've shown me the most amazing thing... just... Baby, I love you, and I gotta get this plugged in because, I gotta. I gotta, Baby. I gotta see this later.

Don't ever let my friends do it. How am I gonna? You gotta make sure. I gotta make sure that I'm gonna get this, please.

People are gonna ask you know... and I gotta make sure I'm getting it. Please. I'm just gonna stop it... just...

And now, so now I'm gonna turn it around, Mama. Instead of watching me, I wanna... Mama. That's you, Baby.

That's you! Oh my God, Mom, you are God. Hmm

Bunn, are you learning from this? You make sure you show people, you got that?

Holy. Okay, I'm gonna use some language that you didn't...

I gotta check the clock, because apparently, I've got forever, and as long as I've got the clock here, to record.

Okay.

Yeah, I gotta make sure, I gotta make sure, as long as I have this with me... when I wake up. Yeah, this is...

Holy! I got you... boom... Jesus. Wow!

Yeah. Where are you, my Mama? Oh.

I'm so sorry, Mama. Hey, I was just checking the clock. I gotta work, and that's not something I want to fuck up, 134. 135. Pretty sure you're still recording. Right?

Get this fucking... listen you fuck. Listen here you fucker. You put the phone down. Now this is for you, and any other mother fucking fuck who wants to use...

Okay, I gotta be quiet.

Don't ever do this drug. If you ever, ever do this drug man... don't you ever do it. Don't you ever... don't you ever, ever, do this you got that?

And you can see me...

Back to my mother, because it's all going to be something you're gonna learn from later fucker. You're recording. Yeah, you're gonna learn from this.

Quiet!

It's only been like, forever, since you know... How long has it been? I'm just checking, because I've got to come back to reality, Mama.

Please, make that be recording. I understand. I'm still good like this is the... I...

Thank you, for letting me come back, Mama. I can never explain this to people. I can never explain it... never explain it.

I am so sorry. Listen Bunn. Listen you fuck. Listen.

Shut up!

Never, Baby... listen okay.

I've been here, as long as it's recording, and if I wake up and this has all just been a fucking dream like... I'm gonna be pissed off.

All right Bunn. You can't ever come back here, again. Are you recording still? 453. I can't imagine that's a hallucination.

Hi sweetheart, Stooge! Can you come here please? Hi baby. Hi. How's it going? Hi.

All right we're done.

Okay, I just want to get you, my love. This is all that matters.

I swear to you, Baby, I died. I died. I'm telling you, now, I died. You don't ever want to do it. I'm telling you. I'm just making sure that I'm putting it on tape.

Please, you don't ever want to do that. You don't. Nope.

You... holy shit... nope! You lose your ego. You lose everything. You cannot... you know...

No no no no don't ever do it again. I promise you people. I hope, Bunn. Listen, listen Bunn. I hope you can figure out a way, Bunn.

Like, this better be recording for fuck sakes. Better be. I better be recording, because if it's not...

You gotta learn from this buddy. Let's check the clock.

If you're coming in, you know there's...

Hi sweetheart. What do you need? Okay.

Mama.

Okay, I'm trying to tell you again. Turn around on me. No, I'm leaving over here.

What about my Daddy, oh my God! Daddy!

Oh Benny! How you doing there, sweet Baby? I'm so sorry too. What a disappointment I've been. I've always...

Are you still getting this? Good it's... you have been disappointed with me, I know. What a piece of shit right?

I understand. You better get it now, bud. When you watch this, don't ever do it again. Don't you fucking ever do it again. Don't you fucking dare.

Learn from this video. I'm starting a new one, just to make sure.

Hi Benny.

I understand, I'm going to be here for like the rest of time. If that's the case... if that's the case...

Can I just live here forever, because it's uncomfortable. It's uncomfortable with my cats, and seeing my dirty, shitty, filthy mess. Look at this. I became that. I became that meth or whatever drug fucking person. I can catch it now... I can catch it now. I can catch it now.

Look, all I hope is, Mama, please. I hope I was quiet.

I'm just a recording away.

I got you, thank you.

Yeah, you're all right. You cats got to stop fighting. Yeah, can you stop fighting, for me? Jesus Christ!

Oh. Checking to see... okay.

I'm going mobile. Okay, so we got worried about cops, because I'm coming too now buddy. I'm looking right at my Mama.   Here, look, you getting this on tape, you fucking idiot? Are you getting this?

You're rocking it back to your own music. That's what you need, because you're going back to work later.

You gotta check on the... you guys, check on... you gotta check on the dipstick here.

Hey, are you in there? Better not be...

Bunn, you just have to learn from this, and don't believe anybody that says you can handle losing yourself, and all that. I promise you... you don't ever want to do it again. Never do it again. Never never ever ever.

Your effects are coming off now and that's good because... are you learning from this?

Why don't you find some fucking eyeglasses? You promise me that you're learning from this. Show me. I need...

You're not going to be recording right? You're not. You won't be. You're gonna be pissed.

Maybe he's still recording one foot around 150.

Listen.   I'm a smart guy, Mom.   I'm gonna start this recording... making a new one again.

Mama, look at me. Don't yell at me. Don't yell at me, Baby. You're teaching me right now...

... because I don't want to go to jail. I don't want to go to jail for something that I will absolutely never ever ever ever ever ever say anybody should do ever never. Nope, I am absolutely against it. I promise you, Bunn, you have to learn from this, and you better be recording it.

If you got all this on tape, that's going to be wonderful.

Let's check the clock. It says quarter to 4. Yep. 346. Is it 346?

Okay, so that was a terrible trip, and unbelievably, it was payment for me being a fucking pig.

I think... okay. Hey I gotta fix...

I love you, Mom. Look at you. Okay, I gotta put this over here, but you learn from this, buddy.

You learn from this, because I'm coming to right now.

All I can do is record this thing, okay. I already promised Mama... okay, I'm turning it over to you. I don't need to see my face. I love you. There you are!

You know what? You came to me tonight. Am I recording this? Yeah, I gotta get you though... no, I have you there. Bunn you have to get you... you have to get...

Gotta make sure it's quiet, because I'm coming to. I got you. It's all about getting the tape for me. I was begging you, at the beginning of the trip.

I'm sorry, Mama. Please be recording. I hope you're recording God damn it. I know this is.

Okay, I swear to God. Huh?

Its recording, thankyou. All right Bunn, and anyone else that sees this... you can never, never do it again.

Wait a second though. If I'm coming back and now I have to reincorporate this into my life... and that's the near-death experience I got... fuck... I got the trip.

I get you, Mama Baby.

I miss you, Baby. I do. I'm just trying to be tough, right? I'm just like, "I don't need anybody. I just plow through the world." It hasn't turned out. Yeah... and look at me.

I tried this drug and, holy fuck, it made me realize that I'm not a very good person. Pretty shitty.

Bunn, are you listening? This is still your Mom talking.

This still better be fucking recording, because I understand that it's 10 to 4, and that's doable.

I love you, Mom, and this experience... yeah, it's gonna change my life. Bunn, okay. I can tell you what to do though, right? Right! Okay, new video.

I'm sure it's real, Mama.

Can you make sure that I just don't get loud? Just make sure I don't get loud.

Just make sure I don't get loud, Mommy.

I want everybody to think.

Morning!

Thank you, and I love you, Mama!

This is coming from your Mom, and it's also coming from you. You learned from this. You got it, and you have the luxury of fixing your life, and I'm gonna do a great job. I understand that Heaven is real, and God, and all that stuff, and I understand that you're there, Baby... your...

Mama, look at you! I understand what I've done wrong, and that's been... I've ignored you.

Mom, please be recording. I gotta make sure because, I've got to learn from this.

You stupid idiot. Would you ever do this again?

Don't you ever do it again. Don't you ever do it... here. Don't you fucking ever do it again.

I'm still with my Mama right now. I'm looking at me, in the video. There. I'm looking at me, there the entire time. I think I've been recording the whole thing. Please, I hope, I hope I did.

I'm sure people come back, and they go all right, but you know what? I'm sitting here, in real life, I got my Mom's pictures up, because she is the only thing that matters.

Ha. I threw, I threw the rest of the drug in the garbage. Oh God, I flushed... I smashed my glass vape in the toilet. That's gonna fucking suck.

I love my little kitty. Hi baby! There's my Stooge doing...

Anyway, Mama, it seems like I have unlimited time here to talk to you, because I really fucked up my life.

Please. Time is moving so fast. Where... no... my God! It's still 5 to 4.

Uh please, please.

Bunn, this is for Bunn, okay? New tape.

Of course, because it's just so important that I make it to work, that's all. I'm gonna make it to work. Look what time is that five to four still? And my speed here is so quick, I'm still watching Stooge there, and I'm sitting here talking to God, who is my Mom.

Are you listening, buddy?

May I play guitar, Mama, while I'm talking to you, Baby? Is that okay? Please, please let me play for you. Bunn, are you recording this, you fucking idiot?

Don't you ever. Life goes on okay. Life will be great, and another hour from now, you'll be like, "well that's over with." Yeah, because you know it's just a DMT trip. You know it's just a DMT trip, right?

You just had the experience. You got the experience.

You got exactly what they all say. You've got that you... you understand why you can't tell people.

But look what happened. Look!

I want to show people. Look. Okay.

That was something that I've done. I have not talked about my Mom. I've kept her in a closet. My Dad too.

He asked... and I didn't get him out. But Mom is God.

Okay. Mom. Are you getting it? Yeah Buddy. Mama is God, and you can never do that drug again. Don't ever do it again. Don't ever ever ever ever. It ruined... it will ruin...

How... I don't know how someone can... I don't know how anybody can say, "Oh, I did the trip, and I'd do it again." Are you fucking kidding me? Bunn! Don't you ever do it. Don't you ever do that.

Okay, I'm gonna start a new tape. These videos will help people. Please. These videos will help people. Please let me get the...

Mama! Look people! Look look look!

You see this beautiful... this beautiful Mama! This is my Mom. She died in 2005. Leukemia. And there's my Dad! You get in too.

My Mom and Dad married. I want to get this, while I have time, but I'm gonna get too sentimental. I don't want to get...

You don't ever want to do this drug, ever.

I'm starting a new... you don't need to start a new tape, you fucking idiot, Jesus Christ... and I love Jesus Christ.

Is the Bible true, Bunn? Is the Bible true?

It kind of is, man. Yeah. Don't forget that, Bunn.

You gotta tell me, Mama. Baby... Mama, you make sure you're recording this please.

Bunn. Yep.

Listen, it's exactly what people always say, okay? Listen, you gotta, you gotta incorporate it back into your life. I'm sure that'll be fine, like you know, I'll be fine, because the trip will end, and uh... I don't think I'll forget it.

Maybe I will... the worst thing ever, Bunn. You died. Now you know that.

But are you getting us on tape? All right. I gotta fix this or come back to reality.

Please, Mama.   These tapes are what's gonna be preventing other people from doing it.   Please, please, allow me to get these recordings. Please.

It's four o'clock now.

This has been a happy experience, and I'll tell you why.

I've learned so much.

Huh? Listen. I fucking died.

I'm sorry, Mama.

I'll never do that drug again. Never, Mommy. I'm still standing here with her, right now. I am, I am.

Mom, am I gonna be fine by work tonight? I'll be good.

I'm gonna make the changes. If I forget this... right. If I forget it, at least it's gonna be on tape, right?

Because if it's not on tape, I'm fucked. I hope I'm smart enough to realize something happened here, and to know to never ever ever never never ever...

I am personally... I'm happy with this. I almost... I better be recording...

I am a strong enough person that I will absolutely be able to incorporate this into my life, Mama. I love you so much. Oh, I love you too, Bubba.

It's been awesome.

Get this on tape, you stupid idiot. Get this on tape. Are you getting this? Fucker, you better be getting this. I hope this isn't part of the hallucinations. Mommy...

Don't you ever do this, I'm not even kidding. I can't put it into words for you, Baby. I can't put it into words for you, Baby.

I love everybody, we're all one.

Look at my Bubba... you're a good boy. I love you, too.

Look, Baby, are you getting this? You better be getting this, you stupid son of a bitch... you stupid son of a bitch. Are you getting this?

You're gonna change your life.

Hey!

It's still recording. So, are you gonna change your life?

That is God. I'm not even kidding you. And don't you ever come here and think you should.

Don't you come here. Do you understand me, Aaron? Keep it down, you gotta keep it down, Mom. You gotta keep it down. You're teaching me here, beautiful. You're teaching me, Baby.

I'm trying to just cover up the volume with my guitar, but you're a little loud, because you're angry... but I got you. I promise you I will never ever ever never...

Is that what you want me to do? Is that what you... yeah, is that what you want me to do? Go against the drug, and teach against it?

I should. I can't tell anybody to do this. I can't, I can't.

I will never hear this. You fucking idiot. How many fucking hours of this have you got? You better have something, you stupid fuck, because if this...

If I find out my phone's fucking blank, I'll be fucking pissed. You're doing this for how long? Fuck, it's another 5 minutes. What's going on? More lessons here for you, Bunn.

You're still sitting here with your Mom... my Mama. I love you, Mama, whatever the volume.

I want to use these tapes. I want to... I'm going to start a new one here, hang on Mama Mama.

I love you, Mama. That's when I was a good boy. That's when I was a good boy. Yeah, that's a good boy. That's when I was a good boy.

Now Bunn, listen. You made a deal with your Mom. You're gonna tell people to never do this journey. Do you understand? You don't want people to come to here. People can't handle it.

Mama, I'm gonna be able to handle it.

Mama, You're still here, Baby.

Are you learning from this? Look at your beautiful Mama. Look at her. You're still sitting with her. She's sitting right here. Right here, right now. Are you listening to me? And you're gonna teach people with this. You're going to teach people, and you're going to tell them to never do it, all right?

You thought you were going to be put in a nut house. You did! Yeah, you thought you were gonna be put in a nut house buddy. You can never do this again, and you can never ever ever allow anybody else to do it.

No Bunn. You're gonna be tempted to do this again. You can never do this drug again. This is your Mother talking.

Just check out the clock, Mama!

I want to help other people not do it.

I can't even believe... this is great! I'm gonna be okay though, because I love you.

Hey, you know what? Oh, it's amazing that it all makes sense! Right! You are God. You... everybody's Mama is God! That is the fact people. That is...

Listen, don't be loud.

That is a fact! Are you listening, Bunn? Listen, look at me. Where the fuck are you... stupid shit.

I am so excited, by the way, Mama. I've been talking to you for hours, and I feel like I've been doing it on the phone here, for hours. And I keep checking reality, and it's 10 after 4... so what am I doing?

It's like an hour long trip now. Like a fucking Ayahuasca or something Mama. I understand that I...

Hi, Baby. I'm looking at my Mama.

I miss you. I'll see you again. I will see you again. It's been so good. I gotta cover up the sound, and fucking turn the TV up. You idiot, shit. It might help you come down, for fuck sakes.

This is only just a bad trip, but don't ever do it again. You gotta promise yourself to never ever. Don't you ever do this again, you stupid son of a bitch.

You're gonna take that vape...

I'm not even fucking interested in drugs, buddy. You can stop your drugs.

I am your Mother. Because I've got time...

Is this all going to be a dream, from my mind? I'm just gonna wake up in my bed? Is that what's gonna happen?

I'm pretty sure this is reality, right here.

Still recording? Good. Bunn, you died tonight.

And you had to admit it. You had to admit you are...

You still watching this? Okay, I gotta have some sound going.

Mom, you stay with me, Baby. Bunn you'll never understand this, and I think you're a human form.

Okay. This is all truth that I'm giving you, here. It's you went to Heaven tonight. You truly did. This is for you to understand. You went to Heaven tonight. It's not a place that you enjoyed, because it's foreign to you.

You were an idiot. You had ignored your beautiful Mama, and that's God. I'm telling you that right now, you stupid son of a bitch. You're gonna get a fucking Bible, for you to read that fucking thing. You got that? Are you getting this?

Maybe, oh. The trip's almost over, Mama.

Bunn, don't you ever do this. Look. Listen don't you ever be...

Listen this is... see your Mama? See? You just spent, you just spent, in fact, she's still here, Bunn. You just spent eternity with her. How do you feel about that, and all I can say is, "It sure beats the shit out of that."

My God, exactly.

Now, don't you. Everything I say in this. Don't let any of it...

I see it, Mama.

I am so sorry.

I'm gonna get the Bible, and read it, and I'm gonna fix my life up, because I understand.

I don't know Jesus. I don't know God. Yes, I understand that I don't understand what's going on over there, because it's all it's exactly what they say.

And it fucks the time and the space... but we can't handle that.

Bunn, say it now. You have to tell anybody you know, to never ever do this drug. Don't you tell them that, "Yeah, you'll go to Heaven, and its awesome."

Bunn, don't you ever do it. Don't you ever do it. You know why? You know why? Look over there. Look over there, on my couch. That's my Mama! Look!

Look, we're not done yet, you stupid son of a bitch.

You tell me, Mom. You tell me. I just checked my watch, beautiful. Just checked my watch, and we're not even done yet.

Mama, please make it... and please...

Please hold your hair. Look at my beautiful Mama.

Now listen to me and listen...

There is absolutely life after death, absolutely.

I spent a long time with my Mother, and your Mama.

My pain. My end. My Dad.

I love them.

I'm not God. Our Mothers are God. I'm telling you that, Aaron. Do you hear me? My Mom keeps coming through me to, tell me this. Are you paying attention?

Mama, you keep telling me. Tell me more. Tell me, okay? Just don't get loud. And at the same time, please make this trip quick and over, because it's fucking 4:30 now, Mama, and I've been a shameful, sack of shit. A terrible person, for doing this.

I'm sorry. I'm sorry that I did it., I'm sorry that... I love you, and it was this... I was a piece of shit Mommy.

I'm happy I got a spiritual trip. Jesus H!

But you killed yourself, Aaron. You took a fucking drug you knew nothing about. And then you over dosed. You never saw it coming, fucker.

Yeah.

Remember when you crossed that line on the staircase? You went right by, and then turned around, and saw that you just over dosed. You were stunned.

You'll never see it coming, Bunn. Don't you ever risk your life... like that again, you shit fuck.

Yep. Everybody's going to be their own piece of shit, and I know what my piece of shit is.

This is so fucking life changing, you stupid fuck.

Here comes my Mom, you stupid fuck, and I can feel her in Me. Mama, I love you, Baby. I'm so sorry, holy shit.

You can't do this ever again. You can't do this ever again. You're gonna fix your fucking life, right? You can't do this again, ever. Don't you ever. Don't.

Are you hearing me? This is your Mother. Don't you ever do this again. You're gonna watch this. You're gonna watch this, you stupid fucking stupid...

You're gonna watch this, and you... this is your Mother... you better, you better, you better never... where's that fucking camera... because you're gonna be looking at my eyes, when you watch this.

I love you Mommy. I love you. It was so good to hang out with you and you're still here... but you're giving me shit, and I fucking deserve it, so you, you go...

I went to heaven tonight, buddy.

I want my Mom, to talk again, because she's still here.

Oh, Mama, please make sure this trip is over for work. Come on, Baby, I mean, I'm looking around the apartment now. I can see everything... hey, what are you guys doing?

I'm gonna try to come back down here. What are you doing here, Stooge? Thank you. I am a little paranoid.

Jesus Christ, even with a babysitter, don't ever do this. In no way, shape, or form, ever do this drug... ever ever ever in your life.

You will be stuck in a fucked plane... moving like this, and you're in there, and time doesn't exist, just like right now. I know you're recording it, Bunn.

Bunn, you have been talking for like a million years, and when you look at your watch, it's now 25 to 5. Now you've learned your lesson, and I'm looking at my Mama, again.

Mama.

And that's the thing. That's the only thing. It's... the only thing I can say is that I'm done with that. Yeah, and I'm never gonna do this drug again. You got that?

I'm still here with my Mom. This is a long ass trip you stupid, fucking, stupid, son of a bitch. Don't you ever take a hallucinogen ever again. Never. You can't handle the truth.

Do you see that? Are you watching this, whoever you are? You watching this, because I'm not out of my mind.

Mom, talk. I want to hear you talk.

I'm still with my Mom, in a place where the time just stands still. ,I love you.

I do not think that anybody should ever do that drug. I hope that people watch these videos.

I am going to tell people.

It's gonna be so hard, because people will say, "What are you talking about, you're fucked! You saw your Mama, and now you know the truth, of life and everything?"

It is really going to be interesting, to see how my life changes, because I am going to change my life, and I promised you, Mama.

Aaron, Aaron, Aaron.

Let's go where I can be a little louder, so I can give you proper God damn shit. Yeah yeah. Let's go, Mom. Come on, we're gonna go. I'll go in here. This is where I should be playing on my beautiful music workstation.

Listen here. Okay I got you, I got you, Mama! I got you. I gotta close the door. I'm okay, Stooge. I'm okay, Stooge.

Okay.

That's my Mama. She is God. I'm telling you the truth. You won't believe me, Bunn, but I got the shit taped, and verified, and I'm pretty proud of that.

And the first life I'm going to change is mine. And the next life that is going to be changed is whoever else is about to try the most terrible thing known in existence.

Don't you ever do that again you stupid, son of a bitch. Don't you ever. Don't you ever, ever do that again you fucking, piece of shit. Did you learn your lesson?

I love you, Mama. I put my phone down. I'm so sorry.

I love you.

It was so good being with you. It was so good. I'm sorry that the fucking part that I had to go through... sorry about the shitty part.

Oh my God, that was so absolutely horrific. I'm so sorry.

I remember, coming to the conclusion that I died. I thought, "I'm dead." This is what happened. I really did think I was dead. I did, I did, I did. Don't do this drug. Don't do it, don't do it, don't do it, nope.

My Mom is still here with us. This is the longest trip. I'm so thankful that I'm getting it on tape, and I don't give a fuck about playing loud music right now. People have to learn from this, and you have to learn from this, you fucking idiot. You tell me Mama. I raised you... I raised you to be a better person.

Hi, Baby, I can't believe it's really you. Bunn, you really are with her, and you believe you still are, but you took way too much of that drug.

Help other people. Be a good boy. I told you that, just before I died. I said, "Be a good boy." You have not been a good boy.

I got it Mom.

Mama, I love you, but could you make this over, please.

I'm gonna live better and... hear it, Aaron. You are going to get a fucking Bible and you are gonna fucking read it because God is real and God is our Mothers, my Mother, everybody's Mother.

That I was punished, for being a piece of shit, and I'm sure there's other people out there that'll have a fucking idea what the fuck I'm talking about, and if you laugh...

I can't imagine.

Sorry. I'm sorry Mom. I love you.

That's not real though. I'll see you again. I love you. Yeah, you're still here. I'm just saying that, because I know that at some point, I'll forget shit.

If you're watching this, and you are a fucking human being, you do not listen to anybody who says that you should do this trip.

Do not, because right now, here right now, I can't handle that bad trip, Jesus Christ! Whoa.

And it's a quadrillion times worse than language can describe.

For me the first half of this was the worst. It's the complete reason why I will never do this again. Bunn, you saw your Mom, you saw your Dad.

You now know that your Mom... oh maybe everybody knows it. But you now know that your Mom is God.

But you're not gonna remember that of course. You won't remember that. People don't remember these things. There was no space Buddy.

But you're gonna be tempted to want to do it again sometimes.

Don't you ever do it again, you hear me? This is silly. This is your fucking Mother talking, can you hear me? She's coming through me now. It's like she just channels through me. I give her a... I allow her to...

Oh, Mommy. Don't make me cry.

Oh that's... sorry, I'm sorry. Oops, I'm pretty sorry. I'm sorry, I'm sorry, I'm sorry, I'm sorry, I'm Amazed.

As much as you might want to come back here, buddy, don't. You found out. You did it. You don't ever need to come back here again. No sweet boy, you don't.

Just remember this. Unfortunately, this fucking trip could go on forever for fuck sakes.

This was all real, but this wasn't in your head. You were... you, you got exactly what people talk about. The ego... you know like it's just...

Won't ever do it again, ever, never Mommy.

Hey, you know what? My Mom is God, and yours is too. And but... you better watch these fucking videos.

Do you understand me?

I know you don't believe me people, it's five to five.

Bunn. Listen. Remember, when he said he was showing you everything, because he knew that nobody would ever believe you? You have to remember what happened on this drug so you can tell people. If you forget it all... you can't tell anybody.

And somehow, I'm still with my Mommy. She is still here. I'm starting to feel a little better, but it was a totally unbelievable... totally believable experience, to be honest with you.

But don't ever do it. Don't you ever do it, again. I won't, Mommy. I love you, and I spent, I've spent so long with you today.

I know what not to do. You gave me shit, and you told me I'm not a good boy... and how did I know that was coming!

But I love you, and I will see you again. It'll be under different circumstances.

Oh yeah.

Its five to five, listen to me, sweetheart.

You stupid, son of a bitch, don't you ever do this drug.

You should have been in a fucking, loony, fucking, farm for this. Don't you ever fuck with your brain again, and psychedelics. Don't you fucking ever do that, ever. Don't you ever do that again. Never do you fucking hear me?

Are you recording?

Don't you ever, ever do psychedelic drugs again, ever. You can't handle the bad trip. You cannot ever risk having that happen again.

Fucking, stupid, fucking, piece of shit... and you better be getting this on a fucking video.

5 o'clock people. Are you fucking stupid, you son of a bitch?

Well, Mom.

I'm taking her with me, okay. Jesus, Bunn, you better learn from all this. You better learn with me. If tonight didn't happen... look at you... look at me.

You can't even show people what your fucking room looks like. You are a fucking disaster. You will never do that drug again. Do you fucking hear me?

Do you fucking hear me? Because...

Like who is this? Is this my Dad? Who is this? Holy shit. I don't know who it is, but it's fucking somebody and then you know... Dad?

I won't, Dad, I won't. I promise, Benny.

Are you hearing me? I don't know who this is. It's not Aaron. You hearing me? You! Are you fucking hearing me? You're hearing me, right?

Yeah.

What the fuck. Don't you ever do this drug again. You better, you better spread the fuckin' word. Don't you ever let anybody else do this drug.

Yeah.

I've apologized so much. I know I'll be fine, because the drug is wearing off. I have to work in six hours.

Just making sure we're still recording here, Mom.

This may end up being something that somebody actually gives a shit about watching, you know.

And I know that there's all kinds of people out there, that are into doing this, and stuff, and if you do, well fine. Well, maybe if you like it go ahead, but Bunn, that's me, don't you ever do it again, you sack of shit. Don't you fucking ever do it again.

Oh, my God, my Mom's still here. I know you don't believe it, but you're watching it, buddy... your gut... goose bumps all through your body right now.

Do you think you have the balls to show this to people?

Yeah. Okay.

Oh, man, I hope one day I can tell people about it. It was crazy, but I'm still hanging out with my Mom.

Oh listen.

Don't you worry at all Baby. Don't you worry at all about life after death. Don't worry at all. Have no fears. Have no fear at all.

Pay attention. That's not me speaking. I'm still in Heaven right now. I am.

They talk rather forcefully from over there, but they are very... I'll let them continue...

The reason Aaron is not going to be doing it anymore is because he died, and spent forever begging for forgiveness from God, and God was his mother, and then She did forgive me, and then She came to my apartment. Right here, right now.

She's still here and it's 10 after 5, and I work in 6 hours.

Right.

So, I need to go, and have a smoke, and let this shit come down, but you know what?

It's been unbelievable, hanging here with you, Mom. Thank you for this wonderful gift. I love you, Baby Baby.

Are we still recording? Gotta check Mom...

end transcript.

I've decided to end the word for word transcript of my conversation there. That's enough. That's all you're gonna get.

There are five more hours of video, capturing my Mother's visit with me. During these hours, she progressively gets more and more angry with me, and it literally tears me apart.

I've presented the first hour or so of conversation, but I'm keeping the rest of it for myself. I hope what I shared with you was an interesting glimpse at what happened when my parents visited me.

My Mom and Dad were there in my apartment for about six hours.

Eventually, Mom was sitting on my couch, and Dad was sitting on a comfy chair. We were just happy to be together.

I sat down at my desktop computer and turned on my web cam to start recording another video of me. While the web cam recorded me, I downloaded all the videos from my phone to my computer.

I was anxious to check the videos. I wanted to see if I caught me dying, on video.

It turns out that I did capture the moment of my death! I tell my parents that, "I got it!" I feel like I have solid proof that something happened to me! Wow!

And then I turn to my parents and realize that their time here is almost up. The fuzzy buzzy feeling is fading away.

"Oh you have to go? This has been the best day of my life. Thank you for this gift, Baby. I love you both so much. I love you, Benny. Thanks for coming with Mom. Thank you for everything you've done for me, Mom. Bye Baby. I'll see you again."

As my parents fade away from my living room, the fuzzy buzzy feeling also disappears along with them.

I sit at my desk, on a small chair, and continue to look through my new video collection. I discover I've captured one mind blowing event after another.

Eventually, I get ready for work and make it to the hotel on time.

CHAPTER 13 - I'M DONE

This book chronicles my eight days of exploring the technique of micro dosing DMT. Chapters Five through Nine represent my first MdDMT experience, while Chapters Eleven and Twelve are my final experience.

This book is what happens if you micro dose DMT.

The first step of a Kundalini experience begins with your base chakra. The process moves upward through an exploration of your own soul. The final step of Kundalini is reaching the top level, the Death Trip.

It begins as a Kundalini Awakening and ends with a Kundalini Cleansing. This is the stairway to heaven. Once you begin ascending it, it will be difficult to stop. This is what leads you to the top, where your soul is finally washed of its filth.

I would like to point out something about the Death Trip that I find very interesting. I want to make sure that everyone caught what happened to me.

Let me take you back to chapter Eleven. Remember when God said to me, "You are reborn." Immediately, I found myself floating at the ceiling of my living room, looking down at myself dying on the couch. My mother was there with me, behind me, while I looked down at myself dying on my couch.

Remember that the next step for me was visiting my parents in their home 'over there'. I found myself hanging out with mom and dad for several hours and we discussed my life, and my mom gave me shit for killing myself with a drug.

Remember that once my visit was over with my parents, I found myself astral projecting back towards my body. Remember there was a small man sitting on a small chair? My soul was returning to that body, the man on the chair. This reconnecting to my body marked the end of the experience and I woke up in my bed.

Now, let's move to the final chapter, where my mom and dad visited me, in my apartment. This event is the exact same Death experience that already happened to me. I experienced the same event twice. It occurred once 'over there' and once 'over here'.

The first time my death happened, I experienced it from the perspective of my soul at the ceiling looking down at me dying on the couch.

I experienced my second death from the point of view of my body, lying on the couch, holding my phone on my chest, talking with my mom. This long conversation lasted hours until I was sitting on a small chair at my computer. This is when my parents left my apartment. This was the end of my second death experience.

Both deaths began with a fuzzy buzzy sensation that continued for the experience and ceased at the end. Both 'deaths' included a several hours long visit with my dead parents. The conversations were mostly identical. I literally said the words I'm wetting myself and shitting myself twice, on two separate occasions. I said it was hilarious twice. I find this very bizarre.

First, I visited them at their place, and then they visited me at my place. This was all in one day. This was the best day of my life, bar none.

I know this all sounds crazy everybody, but I honestly don't care. It is my truth. If you have lost your parents, then you can understand how wonderful this experience must have been for me. From my point of view, I had a ten to twelve hour visit with my parents who both died ten years ago.

Over the years, I've been able to make a lot of sense out of my experience, but I still cannot grasp how I experienced my death twice, each time from the opposite perspective. It will baffle me forever and I'm fine with that.

My Kundalini experience was completely unexpected. I didn't know it would happen when I sat down in my apartment and sipped DMT for the first time. Nobody ever told me what would happen to me. There was no book to teach me what the result of sipping small amounts of DMT would be.

This entire book began as an accident. If I had not set up my camera to record the event, I would have never remembered how it happened to me.

DMT is notorious for wiping a psychonaut's memory clean once the trip ends. Most individuals remember very little at the end of a regular DMT trip. This amnesia did not occur in my case. I emerged from the experience with the ability to recall many of the details.

I would like to remind you of what was said to me in Chapter Six. I was told that 'nobody would ever believe me'. From that moment, I knew that if I could remember the experience once it ends, I would certainly tell others about it. I knew this was something that must be shared with the world.

Well, it turns out that this experience is something that is nearly impossible to share with anyone. This isn't a conversation that can be had over a few coffees. I can't expect someone to sit down and listen to me tell them this book.

And honestly, nobody wants to hear me talking about taking drugs. Obviously, the story begins with drug use. Understandably, finding someone that wanted to hear my story was... impossible.

This left me in a predicament. I knew that I must remember everything so that I could tell someone if they ever wanted to know. I wouldn't allow myself to forget the experience. I replayed this book over and over in my head to ensure that I never forgot it. This is a valuable story, and I knew that if I stopped thinking about it, I would forget it.

These events happened to me in 2016. I am writing this account in 2022. That is more than 2000 days spent replaying this book in my mind. I did it so I wouldn't forget it.

I knew that someday you would come along and be interested in my story. It is a true story. I promise you. I have not lied to you. The fact that you have read my book means that I can finally forget it. This frees me from reliving the experience over and over.

Kundalini is a medicine that is supposed to be used once and then discarded. A cure fixes something. A cure is a process that has a result. A medicine can only be considered a cure if it fixes something, and then you throw away the medicine.

Kundalini is a medicine that you take once. It reminds you of the Truth, and then it self-destructs. Once you learn the Truth, Kundalini extinguishes itself. Kundalini is medicine you only take once.

The effect of a Kundalini Cleansing will stay with you for the rest of your life. There is no need to remember the medicine. You only need to live your new life.

Sharing this book with you means I can finally forget the medicine and just live with the results. Carrying this luggage in my head for six years has been cumbersome. Once I pass this story on to you, I can forget about it and let Kundalini fade away from my memory.

Also, if I forget what happened to me in 2016, I can just read this book.

Do I think other people should try micro dosing DMT for themselves? I suppose a yes or no answer is what many may expect to hear, but I won't reduce this to a one word answer.

I've gone beyond a one word answer. I've presented the entire experience to you. I want *you* to decide if you should try micro dosing DMT. I'm just a human with a great memory and a need to write about it. I can't tell you what to do with your life. I've shown you what happened to me. You are fully capable of making the correct decision yourself. I don't even know you. Or, do I?

This book represents a map or a guide to what happens between lives. I've attempted to take you along with me for the ride. You became my passenger way back in Chapter Four when my lung party happened, and you've been riding along with me ever since.

Together, we made it through the book. As we approach the end of the trip, there are a few things I would like to say.

I haven't forgotten about the title of this book, believe me. There is a time and place for everything.

Our ride together is almost over, and I hope I have prepared you to some extent for what you are going to find at the end of this trip.

You won't expect it unless someone has already told you how this experience ends.

You should really like the ending. Truly, it should make you very happy.

The problem is that you won't believe it, even if you want to. This will be so opposite of what you've been taught by language, history, culture, and tradition etc.

Let's face it. You don't ever need to micro dose DMT. You don't have to believe a word in this book. You can throw this writing away if you hate it, but I promised you at the start of all this that I would tell you the Truth. I can't stop now because we're almost done, and you're still with me. You might as well go all the way.

Let me say thank you to you. You are the real reason I wrote this. Thank you for buying my book of course, but most importantly, thank you for coming along with me for the ride. I hope you have found some value in reading this crazy book. Perhaps you won't need to try MdDMT for yourself. You can experience the cure without the trip. All you have to do is believe what I'm about to tell you.

I am about to arm you with the ability to see the world with a new set of eyes. You will be able to separate the truth from the lies.

My work is almost done. It's all up to you now my friend. You either believe it, or you don't. If you believe it, then you are cured. It really is as simple as that.

You have lived many lives before this one. That thing that sits between your ears and behind your eyes and thinks about everything... that's your soul. You have been that soul forever. Your soul has never closed its eyes. Even over the course of millions of separate lives, your soul is really having one, long, uninterrupted experience.

Every life you have ever lived has ended with a Kundalini Cleansing.   You live a life, you die, you experience Kundalini, and without fail you are reborn.

This is how it has always been. This is reincarnation.

Don't fear reincarnation. It is actually a gift from your Mother. You see, you've never been taught the Truth about where you are. I know that language, history, culture, and tradition have led you to believe that you are somewhere that you are not. Cherish reincarnation. Do not wish to escape it.

The last time you died, you were let into Heaven. That's the Truth. Each and every life you've lived over millions of years, has ended with you being allowed into Heaven.

There is no other place. There is only Heaven.

Your Mother loves you unconditionally. She has never denied you entry to Heaven.

As a soul, you are either here living a life in Heaven, or you are experiencing a Kundalini cleansing. Those are the two 'places' a soul can be.

This *is* the Garden of Eden. Who told you it wasn't? Look around at the world. Take away the people, and you're left with the Garden of Eden. The Garden has always been here, since the very beginning. This is the only place you are ever born. You have never been born anywhere else but here, in Heaven.

Your Mother gives birth to you in Heaven every time. You have never been born anywhere else. That is how much She loves you.

It is very unfortunate that we don't have signs here welcoming babies to Heaven. From the baby's point of view, he/she was just let in through the Pearly Gates. This should be the most wonderful place ever for the baby.

From day one, the enlightened little mind of the new baby is overwritten with information that eventually results in an adult that has no memory of the Truth that they knew as a baby. Babies are new and physically fragile, but the soul inside a baby possesses the memory of its very recent Kundalini Cleansing. Infinite wisdom lies between the ears and behind the eyes of a baby.

It would be wonderful if the world simply taught babies where they are. Carry this education on through to adulthood. Teach the Truth and after a few generations, the world would literally be Heaven on earth.

The idea that we live here, and there is Heaven above and Hell below... that is pure nonsense. Don't fall for it.

Do not fear death at all. Your Mother loves you unconditionally. She will never judge you. However, you will judge yourself. You too will stand on that path in a clearing in a forest for days, trying to delay the inevitable. You will judge your own behaviour as a human. You will demolish your own ego with your apologies. You too will reduce yourself to a pile of dirty, filthy, bricks.

And as always, once you have absolutely exhausted yourself with apologies, your ever-loving Mother will scoop you up, clean you off, and give you a new human interface so that you may experience Heaven, again and again. Your soul never dies, but once in a while, it needs a new body.

It will be your own personal list of apologies that will be your undoing. You will judge yourself. God stays out of it until you are done tearing yourself apart. Your best bet is to show up there on the path, with the shortest list possible. The shorter your list of apologies, the less you will suffer from your own behaviour. When it is over, God will wash the filth off you, issue you a replacement body, and send you back to Heaven. Back to here, regardless of where you have been told *this* is.

Every human has arrived here through their Mother's vagina. That is the only entry to the Garden. It always has been that way since the beginning of time. Everyone enters Heaven through their Mother's vagina. Humans do not grow from rib bones.

Doesn't any of this make sense?

You are always in Heaven my friend. You made it to the Garden, again. You've never existed anywhere else. You've been given the ultimate gift of unconditional love, over and over again. Please recognize that.

It is up to you to make this place a better place while you are here. You will be coming right back to whatever world you leave behind for yourself.

You may be a King or Queen today, but you also may be a peasant when you come back. Make the world better for the peasants, not yourself. You probably will be a peasant next time.

That is karma. If you shit in the Garden when you're here, it will be a shitty Garden when you return.

Spend more time celebrating that you are already in Heaven. Be amazed that you are in the Garden of Eden.

Love Mother Nature, for real. Don't fake it. Don't be a liar.

Help Our Mother take care of this place. Have respect for where you are.

This is Heaven for YOU if you realize it, but it's Hell for YOU if you don't.

Don't take life too seriously. You've done it all before. There really isn't anything you *need* to accomplish in this life.

Spend more time in The Garden with your Mother. Love and protect this place. Acknowledge Her existence. Thank Her once in a while.

Real eyes realize real lies. Identify the lies and ignore them completely. Teach others the Truth when you find it.

Be courageous and tell people.

And always love and respect your Mother.

The time will come, sometime in the distant future, when my sweetheart and I will lie down together in bed. After we entertain our cats for a while, we will turn off the light. She will say I love you, and I will say I love you too baby. I'll give her a kiss on her beautiful cheek and tuck myself in behind her.

Maybe I'll dream. I don't dream often, but occasionally I like to run through farmer's fields, in the moonlight. I take huge bounding jumps and rise hundreds of feet in the air before coming down to the ground, only to do it again.

Perhaps from a dream, I will awaken suddenly. My eyes will pop open in the darkness of our bedroom.

I will know what is happening to me. I'll be able to feel the fuzzy buzzy sensation all around me. Of course, I'll know what it is. I've been expecting it since I was 49 years old.

I will think about my sweetheart who is still happily asleep beside me. I'll realize that her life is about to change. I'll think about my cats and how they will miss me.

But my thoughts will eventually turn to the fuzzy buzzy energy that is coming for me.

I know it won't be long before my Mother arrives. She is always there when I die. This time will be no different.

And then it will happen as it always happens. She will say "Don't be scared." and then take my hand to lead me through my next Kundalini Cleansing.